AIRCRAFT OF THE ACES

133

Ju 88 ACES OF WORLD WAR 2

SERIES EDITOR TONY HOLMES

133

AIRCRAFT OF THE ACES

Robert Forsyth

Ju 88 ACES OF WORLD WAR 2

OSPREY
PUBLISHING

OSPREY PUBLISHING
Bloomsbury Publishing Plc

Kemp House, Chawley Park, Cumnor Hill, Oxford OX2 9PH, UK
29 Earlsfort Terrace, Dublin 2, Ireland
1385 Broadway, 5th Floor, New York, NY 10018, USA
Email: info@ospreypublishing.com
www.ospreypublishing.com

OSPREY is a trademark of Osprey Publishing Ltd

First published in Great Britain in 2019

A catalogue record for this book is available from the British Library.

Print ISBN: 978 1 4728 2921 4
ePub: 978 1 4728 2922 1
ePDF: 978 1 4728 2923 8
XML: 978 1 4728 2924 5

Edited by Tony Holmes
Cover artwork by Mark Postlethwaite
Aircraft profiles by Jim Laurier
Index by Alan Rutter
Originated by PDQ Digital Media Solutions, UK
Printed and bound in India by Replika Press Private Ltd.

22 23 24 25 26   10 9 8 7 6 5 4

The Woodland Trust
Osprey Publishing supports the Woodland Trust, the UK's leading woodland conservation charity.

www.ospreypublishing.com
To find out more about our authors and books visit our website. Here you will find extracts, author interviews, details of forthcoming events and the option to sign-up for our newsletter.

ACKNOWLEDGEMENTS
The author would like to extend his thanks to Dénes Bernád, Eddie J Creek, Roger Gaemperle, Chris Goss, Tony Holmes, Claire Rose Knott, Prinz Alexander zu Sayn-Wittgenstein, Dave Wadman and John Weal for their kind assistance with this book.

Front Cover
On 13 August 1943, Oberleutnant Dieter Meister of 13./KG 40, flying a Ju 88R-2 coded F8+NX, shot down a Wellington XIII of No 304 'Polish' Sqn that was on sea patrol searching for U-boats in the Bay of Biscay. Twenty-four-year-old Meister had joined V./KG 40 from bomber training school in July 1942. Wellington HZ638, coded 2P, had taken off from its base at Davidstow Moor, in Cornwall, at 0936 hrs. Its crew of Flt Lt S Widanka, Plt Off S Kielan and Sgts W Pastwa, L Dangel, F Gorka and K Czarnecki were all posted missing. The 13 August encounter was at least Meister's second with the Poles of No 304 Sqn, for on 16 October 1942 his Ju 88C-6 had been damaged by another of the unit's Wellingtons, although he and his crew had escaped unhurt. Serving in both 13. and 15. *Staffeln*, Meister was awarded the *Deutsches Kreuz in Gold* on 17 October 1943. That same month V./KG 40 was redesignated I./ZG 1 and Meister was appointed *Kapitän* of 3. *Staffel*. He is believed to have been credited with ten victories by war's end.
(*Cover artwork by Mark Postlethwaite*)

CONTENTS

INTRODUCTION

On the grey, rain-swept evening of 16 March 1940, the Royal Navy's Home Fleet anchorage at Scapa Flow in the Orkney Islands was occupied by no fewer than five large warships. The battlecruiser HMS *Hood* and battleship HMS *Valiant* had arrived at Scapa on the 7th, while the battleship HMS *Rodney* and battlecruisers HMS *Repulse* and HMS *Renown* entered the Flow two days later. The anchorage and the ships lying in it had been the subject of attention from the Luftwaffe since the previous autumn, with generally small-scale nuisance and probing bombing attacks being mounted on a regular basis. But now there was an increasing sense of urgency about the destruction of these ships, for at the beginning of the month Adolf Hitler had issued his directive for *Fall Weserübung* – the invasion of Denmark and Norway.

The official record of the *Kriegsmarine*'s Naval Staff Operations Division encapsulates the circumstances;

'The striking concentration on 10/11 March of British heavy ships in Scapa, which is still greatly endangered from the air, combined with other reports received, makes a landing operation in Norway by a Franco-British Expeditionary Corps, with the aid of the entire British Home Fleet, seem perfectly possible as early as the week of 11-16 March.'

Obviously, any such risk had to be prevented at all costs if the success of *Weserübung* was to be assured. Aside from the despatch of U-boats, the dropping of mines and the flying of reconnaissance missions over

Major Fritz Doench (right), *Gruppenkommandeur* of I./KG 30, discusses his unit's attack on the Royal Navy anchorage at Scapa Flow on 16 March 1940 at a press reception a few days after the high-profile mission, which, although alarming the British, did not achieve its intended results. Doench, who would be decorated with the Knight's Cross on 19 June 1940, is seen here pointing at a map of the naval and airfield targets at Scapa Flow with Oberleutnant Hunno Phillipps (left) of I./KG 26 and Oberleutnant Helgo Magnussen of 3./KG 30. Phillipps was killed in action on the night of 19/20 November 1940 when his He 111 caught on a balloon cable and crashed in southern England while on a raid to Birmingham, and Magnussen perished when his Ju 88A-2 crashed at Oudenrijn, in the Netherlands, on 10 May 1940 the Orkneys and Shetland areas, a further measure considered necessary was, 'Bombing attacks on the British heavy ships lying in Scapa, using very strong attacking forces'. The problem with this for the Luftwaffe was the paucity of aircraft fast enough, and with the required range, to get in and out of the target area quickly with sufficient bomb load to impart significant damage.

So it was that as a window opened in the rain and snow showers, away to the northeast of Scapa Flow a group of 18 aircraft appeared in the fading light on the horizon. These were Junkers Ju 88A-1 *Schnellbombers* of I./KG 30 operating as part of X. *Fliegerkorps* from their advanced airfield at Westerland, just over 500 nautical miles to the east, on the German island of Sylt. The Junkers bombers would form one prong of the attack, directed against the ships, while sixteen He 111s of KG 26 were assigned to strike at three identified airfields. In fact, the combined force would be depleted as a result of five aircraft breaking off with technical problems. Leading the small formation of Ju 88s was *Gruppenkommandeur* Major Fritz Doench, known to his crews as 'Uncle Fritz'.

The Ju 88 was regarded as the most advanced bomber aircraft in the world at the time, but of the 64 machines available to the whole of the *Geschwader*, only 22 were operationally ready. Powered by two supercharged 1200 hp Junkers Jumo 211B-1 12-cylinder, liquid-cooled, fuel-injected engines which produced a maximum speed of 450 km/h at an altitude of 5500 m, the Ju 88A-1 could, on paper, carry an internal bomb load of 1400 kg, comprised of 28 50-kg SC-50 bombs. Put another way, the aircraft could carry 500 kg of bombs for 3677 km with fuel tanks full, but on shorter missions of up to 1260 km, it could carry 2400 kg of bombs. The crew of four was protected by a pilot-operated, windscreen-mounted 7.9 mm MG 15 machine gun. Two further such guns were mounted in the rear of the cockpit and at the rear of a ventral fuselage gondola.

Some of KG 30's crews were among the best the Luftwaffe could offer, specially trained for anti-shipping missions while serving with the original Ju 88 operational trials unit, *Erprobungskommando* 88, although there had still been relatively little 'serious' action from the time missions had started in September 1939. These initial attacks on enemy warships over the North Sea and the coast of Scotland, which included targeting the aircraft carrier *Ark Royal*, as well as a number of British cruisers, were devised by the officer pilots, and more permanent tactics would be established based upon them. Therefore, at the time of the Scapa Flow mission of 16 March, although he had already flown several such sorties against the British naval base, Doench was effectively making up his own methods of attack, this time with 1000-kg SD 1000 bombs.

Doench had first entered military service with the *Reichswehr* in October 1923 as an artilleryman, before commencing flying training at the secret German base at Lipetzk, in the Soviet Union, when the terms of the Versailles Treaty were still very much in effect. He qualified as a pilot and joined the new Luftwaffe in 1935 with the rank of Hauptmann, opting to fly bombers. Promoted to Major, Doench was assigned to the *Luftwaffen-Lehrdivision* (Development and Operational Training Division) at Greifswald.

Shortly after the outbreak of war, on 16 October 1939, Doench had taken over command of I./KG 30 from Hauptmann Helmut Pohle, who had been shot down by Spitfires off the coast of Scotland but survived to be taken prisoner, the *Gruppe* having been established at Jever from I./KG 25 only the month before.

As Doench led his Ju 88s towards the waters of Scapa Flow at 1950 hrs, they were greeted by a barrage of anti-aircraft fire, and the crews could make out the hazy grey shapes of the warships ahead of them. Doench ordered his formation to break up into *Ketten* – or elements of three aircraft – instructing the crews to select individual targets for their bombs, before turning into a steep dive from 2000 m. Prime targets were *Rodney* and *Renown*.

'Everything went like clockwork', Doench subsequently recalled. 'We had achieved complete surprise and were able to plant our bombs with great accuracy. Several ships received direct hits. Others suffered near misses, which must have caused severe damage'.

At 2010 hrs the German crews turned back across the North Sea to return to Westerland, elated by their apparent success. After landing, Doench and his men reported scoring two hits on a battleship, one hit on a battleship or battlecruiser, one hit on a battlecruiser and one hit on a heavy cruiser, while two bombs were dropped in the immediate vicinity of further battleships so that damage was assumed. The Naval Staff Operations Division noted jubilantly;

'The X. *Fliegerkorps* has achieved excellent results in the successful attacks on Scapa. Detailed results cannot be checked for the present. According to available reports there is no doubt of some severe and some moderate damage to battleships or heavy cruisers. The ship hit by two 1000-kg bombs must be claimed as out of action for some time.'

The *Gruppe's* only casualty was a Ju 88 of 3. *Staffel* that became lost and crashed onto a Danish island in the Baltic – a small price to pay for such results. The reality, however, was very different, for the attack was a military failure. Only the cruiser HMS *Norfolk* suffered any significant damage, being holed under the waterline, while the depot ship HMS *Iron Duke* was lightly damaged from three near misses. Nevertheless, the raid did carry the infamous distinction of being the first to inflict civilian casualties in the British Isles. The Admiralty also became so worried about the threat of German air attack following this raid by the Luftwaffe's new high-speed bombers that the Home Fleet was ordered to sea during the next moonlight period.

However, swept along on a tide of mistaken self-belief and optimism, the Luftwaffe *had* scored one major success – propaganda. In the Third Reich, like the fearsome Junkers Ju 87 Stuka dive-bomber that had been unleashed to terrifying effect in Poland, the Ju 88 *Schnellbomber*, able to perform the roles of both conventional and dive-bomber, was regarded confidently as another shining symbol of Nazi technical accomplishment and superiority. Yet the truth was another matter, for the much vaunted Ju 88A-1 was plagued by several major problems. The highly stressed build of the aircraft meant that a pilot had to use the slatted underwing dive-brakes with caution, avoiding too much violent manoeuvring – a curious shortcoming given that the aircraft was seen as a dive-bomber. The Ju 88's undercarriage had also proven rather less robust than had been hoped for, resulting in bomb loads having to be accommodated exactly in accordance with factory instructions. It was a sensitive aircraft.

In recognition of Doench's 'exploits' over Scapa Flow, four days after the raid he was awarded the Iron Cross First Class. Subsequently, he would become an early recipient of the *Ritterkreuz* (Knight's Cross), which was awarded on 19 June 1940 following successes achieved by I./KG 30 during the Norwegian and French campaigns. As the war progressed, Doench would be appointed to various staff positions within II. *Fliegerkorps* and the *Reichsluftfahrtministerium* (RLM – German Air Ministry) prior to his death on 14 June 1942 during a dive-bombing exercise in Italy while at the controls of a Ju 88A-4.

The legacy of those early missions against the Royal Navy was to introduce to the world the Ju 88, a *Schnellbomber* that would go on to serve the Luftwaffe as a revered multi-role day and night combat aircraft. As a bomber, more than 15,000 examples were built, making it the most widely produced aircraft of its type in the Luftwaffe inventory. It would also be the aeroplane in which the glittering careers of many pilots would be made. Fritz Doench had been one of the first.

CHAPTER ONE

SCHNELL ... SCHNELL ... SCHNELL ...

There is no question that the Ju 88 was one of the most effective aircraft of World War 2 – its multi-mission track record speaks for itself. The sleek Ju 88A-1, which, just from its appearance, suggested 'speed', had evolved from a series of prototypes designed during the 1930s by a formidable team of designers and engineers at the Dessau-based Junkers Flugzeug und Motorenwerke under the leadership of Dipl.-Ing. Ernst Zindel. They had responded to a 1934 requirement from the RLM for a multi-role and heavily armed *Kampfzerstörer* (best translated as 'combat destroyer') that would be able to fly bomber, reconnaissance and ground-attack missions.

Just months later, however, the RLM revised its requirement as it was envisaged that, realistically, such an aircraft would be tagged as *'Es kann alles, aber nichts davon richtig'* ('Jack of all Trades, but a Master of None'). Thus, the requirement was focused towards a *Schnellbomber* (fast bomber) with a crew of three, which would be able to climb to 7000 m in 25 minutes, fly at a maximum speed of 500 km/h and carry a maximum bomb load on horizontally-mounted racks of 1000 kg to a range of around 2000 km. The aircraft was to be ready quickly – by August 1935. To ensure

Factory-fresh Ju 88A-1 Wk-Nr 3134 9K+EL shortly after its delivery to 3./KG 51 in France in May 1940. I. *Gruppe* had started to replace its He 111s with Ju 88s from the previous month speed in performance, the *Schnellbomber* would be either unarmed or carry the minimum armament, in the belief that with such power and lightness, it would easily be able to evade attack from any enemy fighter.

The tender for such a specification was put out to Focke-Wulf, Henschel, Junkers and Messerschmitt. The August 1935 deadline came and went, with work finally commencing on prototypes in May 1936. What emerged from the Zindel team was a twin-engined, low-wing design with a single fin and rudder, with the crew accommodated in a 'greenhouse' cockpit positioned well forward and housed beneath a canopy that was almost flush with the fuselage. The ailerons and flaps were aligned with the wing trailing edges, with the power coming from a pair of 1000 hp Daimler-Benz DB 600A 12-cylinder, liquid-cooled engines housed in neat, slim nacelles.

The first all-metal, stress-skinned prototype, the Ju 88 V1, took to the air from the Dessau works on 21 December 1936 and was followed through to 1938 by a short series comprising the V2 to the V5. Progressively, this series saw the incorporation of a single 7.9 mm MG 15 machine gun (although like the V1, the V2 was unarmed), with bombs being loaded under the wings for testing. The DB 600A was soon replaced by the 'in-house' Junkers-manufactured 1000 hp Jumo 211A. Despite the loss of the V3 in a crash on 24 February 1938 while attempting to carry a load of 2000 kg (the crew of two were killed), the Ju 88 had already been given the thumbs-up by RLM test pilots at the *Erprobungsstelle* Rechlin.

At this point, the competing firms eased out of the tender and Junkers was officially awarded the task of building the *Schnellbomber*. On 3 September 1938, Generalfeldmarschall Hermann Göring told Dr Heinrich Koppenberg, the head of Junkers, 'Go ahead and give me a great bomber fleet of Ju 88s in the shortest possible time!'

Indeed, so elated and confident was the head of the *Technisches Amt*, Generalmajor Ernst Udet, with Junkers' work on the Ju 87 dive-bomber that in November 1937 he had ordered that the Ju 88 should also be built with dive-bombing capability, thus adding another major requirement to its 'multi-role' demands. Not surprisingly, Zindel brought in his colleague, Dipl.-Ing. Hermann Pohlmann, who had worked on the Stuka, to incorporate a dive-brake system into the Ju 88 so as to ensure the aircraft would be able to pull out safely from dives.

By the time the fifth prototype made its inaugural flight on 13 April 1938, the aircraft was fitted with Jumo 221B-1 engines with four-bladed propellers. The V5 was subsequently modified by the removal of its ventral, 'bathtub'-shaped gondola and its previously glazed nose made unglazed, with the cockpit glazing being lowered to increase streamlining. In this configuration, in March 1939, the aircraft attained an average speed of 517 km/h over a distance of 1000 km while carrying 2000 kg, establishing a new closed-circuit record. The crew of the Ju 88 had also increased to four in a standard configuration.

The Ju 88 V6, which had first flown on 18 June 1938, served as the prototype for the ensuing A-0 and A-1 series. As well as four-bladed propellers, the fuselage had been lengthened, there were two internal bomb-bays, larger horizontal tail surfaces and significantly redesigned landing gear that retracted hydraulically rather than electrically and which rotated 90 degrees to lie flat with the nacelles. Ten Dessau-built pre-production A-0s were assigned to the testing and evaluation unit *Erprobungskommando* 88, while the A-1 was used operationally in relatively small numbers by the Luftwaffe (see Introduction) and fitted with three-bladed propellers. By the end of 1939, 69 Ju 88A-1s had been built at Dessau, but plans were put in place to expand and disperse production to a range of other Junkers and third-party plants from 1940.

When flying the Ju 88, the pilot benefitted from excellent forward and downward visibility, the latter aspect being improved by the semi-circular layout of the instruments and from a canopy that had been raised to improve crew comfort. The bomb-aimer would operate his sight, which was mounted in the 'beetle's eye' nose made of 20 optically-flat Plexiglas panels. Armament would comprise a single, pilot-operated, forward-firing MG 15 in the right side of the cockpit windscreen (known as the A-*Stand*), while such weapons were also installed, initially, in the rear of the cockpit (B-*Stand*) and in the rear of the ventral gondola, known as the *Bola* (C-*Stand*). In the *Bola*, the fourth crewmember would lie prone to use the gun, which provided rearward and downward arcs of defensive fire. The rear cockpit armament would later be doubled. While there was very little armour protection to save on weight, the crew could at least draw linen sun blinds to prevent glare and heat.

Fuel was carried in non-metallic, self-sealing wing tanks, one outboard of each nacelle and one inboard, with a capacity in each wing of 840 litres. An ordnance load of 28 five-kilogram bombs could be carried internally, while carriers inboard of the engines could each carry a 500-kg bomb, although it was normal to carry only two 100-kg bombs when the internal bay was fully loaded.

On missions that would involve dive-bombing, the pilot, after sighting his target, would lower the dive brakes, with hydraulic pressure being applied to one side of a piston that moved the elevator servo tab to the dive position. The dive commenced, usually at an angle of 50-60 degrees. Once the bombs had been dropped electrically at around 1000 m, the elevator trim would reset to enable safe recovery, after which the pilot would retract the dive brakes manually as the aircraft levelled out.

Following with some delay from the A-1, the A-2 (Jumo 211G engines for RATO fitment and heavy loads) and the A-3 (dual-control trainer), came the Ju 88A-4 in early 1940, which saw some major design improvements over the A-1. These included, primarily, the fitment of the new Jumo 211J rated at 1350 hp, which had finally become available, and an extended wingspan of 20.08 m from 18.25 m. A number of A-1s had also been modified to A-4 standard by featuring the new wing, becoming A-5s in the process – a variant that actually preceded the A-4 marginally when examples were delivered in the spring of 1940. Nevertheless, it would be the A-4 that would go on to equip many Luftwaffe bomber and reconnaissance units, and remain in service for the entire war, earning itself a formidable reputation.

However, when Germany invaded Poland in September 1939, among the Luftwaffe's Order of Battle was just one available *Staffel* of Ju 88s. I./KG 25 was established with around 18 Ju 88A-0s and A-1s at Rechlin effectively as a redesignation of the assessment unit *Erprobungskommando* 88. Although on paper a *Gruppe*, in reality only a *Staffel*-strength unit could be raised

A crew member of a Ju 88 of the *Stab* of KG 30 signals from his aircraft's cockpit. The bomber is adorned with the famous diving eagle emblem of the *'Adler' Geschwader*, the bird set against a shield of red, white and yellow Pales, or stripes

(under the command of Hauptmann Helmut Pohle) from what was taken on from the *Kommando*. The short-lived I./KG 25 was redesignated I./KG 30 on 22 September, and it is possible that some Ju 88s conducted brief operations over Poland. Pohle transferred to the new *'Adler' Geschwader* as *Kommandeur* of I. *Gruppe*, but was succeeded by Fritz Doench on 16 October 1939 when the former was made a PoW after being shot down.

Commencing 21 September 1939, I./KG 30's main role was to attack the ships of the Royal Navy in the North Sea, although most of the *Gruppe* had been withdrawn inland from Jever, on the North Sea coast, to Greifswald and Hagenow. Nevertheless, on 26 September, the Ju 88 would make its first claim to fame when a 'lowly' Gefreiter, a certain Carl Francke, flying in a formation of four Ju 88s led by Leutnant Walter Storp, launched an audacious dive-bombing attack against the aircraft carrier HMS *Ark Royal*.

There was more to Francke than met the eye. The Gefreiter had volunteered for service with *Erprobungskommando* 88, where Pohle was an old friend. Francke had actually joined the *Gruppe* from Rechlin, the experienced aviator having flown as a member of the German team – led by World War 1 fighter ace Theo Osterkamp – competing in the *Europa-Rundflug* air race in 1934. In the summer of 1937, while Head of Department E7 at the *Erprobungsstelle*, Francke had also flown the Bf 109 V8 and V13 prototypes in award-winning high-speed and climb-and-dive flights at the 4th International Flying Meeting at Dübendorf, in Switzerland.

As a member of the Luftwaffe he had served as a test pilot at the *Erprobungsstelle (See)* at Travemünde, where he had made a name for himself by being heavily involved in testing both seaplanes and new types of fighter, and compiling the standard manual for flight-testing. Francke had also test-flown the Ju 88 on numerous occasions. Transferring to Rechlin, he would fly the first prototype of the He 177 heavy bomber in November 1939, as well as more 'exotic' types such as the Focke-Wulf Fw 61 V2 autogyro and the Messerschmitt 321, the world's largest glider.

On 26 September 1939, Francke was on Sylt as a member of the small KG 30 *Bereitschaftskette* (readiness section) under the command of Storp that had been detached to the island. Following the receipt of reconnaissance reports, the Ju 88s took off just after 1300 hrs and headed out across the sea at an altitude of just 500 m so that the observation of enemy vessels would be easier. When the warships were sighted, including an aircraft carrier, Francke climbed to 3000 m, passing above the cloud layer, with the intention of making a diving attack. However, this meant that the carrier, which he had targeted, would not be visible as he commenced his dive. As he later recalled, 'On breaking back down through the cloud, it was immediately apparent that the attack would not be successful'.

Ark Royal had slipped out of Francke's sights. At approximately 1345 hrs the battleship *Rodney* had picked up two or three groups of aircraft on its Type 79Y radar at a range of approximately 80 miles and closing.

Francke wasted no time and climbed back up into the cloud to prepare for a second attempt. As he re-emerged a few minutes later, he flew into a hail of anti-aircraft fire from *Ark Royal*. At 2700 m he began his dive, making small adjustments until he was directly over the target, explosions bursting in the sky around him. Remarkably, he was not hit, and he released his SD-500 bombs. He watched as the first exploded in the water some 20 m away from the carrier, while the second seemed to strike the ship's starboard side. As he pulled away, Francke's radio operator, Unteroffizier Bewermeyer, saw a fountain of water close to the carrier and then observed thick black smoke and flames climbing skyward.

Major Walter Storp, photographed while *Kommodore* of SKG 210 in Russia, is wearing the Oak Leaves to the Knight's Cross that he was awarded on 14 July 1941. Earlier in the war, he had shown his prowess as a Ju 88 dive-bomber pilot when he launched several attacks on enemy warships while with I./KG 30 and III./KG 4, including targeting a 10,000-GRT troop transport at Dunkirk. He would fly the Ju 88 once again when *Kommodore* of KG 6

The reality, however, was that Francke's second bomb had narrowly missed its target by just five metres off the port bow, sending a violent column of white water avalanching across *Ark Royal*'s flightdeck and lifting the carrier upwards. Its commanding officer, Capt Arthur Power, had moved the vessel away from the falling bomb just in time. The carrier initially began to list to starboard, although it eventually righted itself.

Elsewhere, Walter Storp had attacked the battlecruiser *Hood*, with one of his bombs simply bouncing off its quarter plating and only stripping off paint when it failed to explode. The remaining Ju 88s made high-level attacks from 3500 m, but to no effect. To the British, the attacks appeared uncoordinated, and no attempt was made to focus especially on the carrier. Equally, however, the Commander-in-Chief of the Home Fleet, Adm Sir Charles Forbes, commented that his gunners had been 'obviously unprepared for such high-performance dive-bombing.'

A subsequent post-raid reconnaissance flight despatched to investigate spotted two battlecruisers but no aircraft carrier. Despite some initial scepticism on the part of the Luftwaffe Chief of General Staff, Generaloberst Hans Jeschonnek, and other senior officers, the RLM in Berlin hastily concluded that the Ju 88s had done exactly what was required of them and had sunk the *Ark Royal*. On the 30th, the *Luftwaffenführungsstab* proclaimed jubilantly, 'From the observations of the Ju 88s which attacked the aircraft carrier, it can be seen that the thick-walled SD-500-kg bombs with delay fuses exploded the fuel tanks within the carrier (flames and clouds of black smoke). Even small air formations (13 aircraft) are capable of inflicting serious damage on heavy naval forces'.

After the raid, a decidedly uncomfortable Francke protested to Pohle about the exaggerated and incorrect claims being rolled out by Berlin, but it would be to no avail. A little later a telegram arrived at Westerland from none other than Generalfeldmarschall Göring congratulating Francke for his 'outstanding bravery' and awarding him the Iron Cross Second and First Classes, to which was added promotion to Leutnant. The propaganda machine was unstoppable and the Ju 88 was now viewed by Göring as a 'Wunderbomber'. The luckless Leutnant Franke would be briefly posted to 3./KG 30 before returning to work at Rechlin. His 'supposed' sinking of the Ark Royal would haunt him for a long time to come.

For the rest of the year and into early 1940, KG 30 maintained operations against the British Home Fleet and its bases at Scapa Flow, the Firth of Forth and along the English coast. Successes were few and far between, but the Ju 88s did sink the minesweeper HMS Sphinx off the Moray Firth on 3 February as part of wider-scale Luftwaffe attacks on shipping between Rattray Head and Cromer – an event which was followed six days later by the sinking of two minesweeping trawlers off Aberdeen, although one Ju 88 was lost as well.

One officer of 3./KG 30 described what it was like to fly a frustrating mission to Scapa on 8 March 1940;

'The few missions that were flown were usually flown in "Kette" formation, as was this failed mission to Scapa Flow. I was still a member of 2. Staffel at this time and was accompanied by another Oberleutnant from this Staffel as well as Hielscher from 3. Staffel.

'We flew at an altitude of 4000-5000 m over the North Sea and produced heavy condensation trails as we neared the Orkney Islands. Our approach had been distant from the Scottish coastline, and as a result enemy fighters did not bother us. That was true even as we approached the target area. As we approached the target, we could not make out large warships or naval units – not around the surrounding islands or in the great bay of Scapa Flow. Since we had a long flight behind us we had little fuel left to start a major search, and attacked the small boats that floated around below us. My bombs were aimed at a harbour patrol boat and missed. Our leader had picked a training ship, but was shot down by fighters that we had noticed as we had initiated our attack. Our third aircraft also was unsuccessful. After we landed, we found out that he had technical problems. In short, this was a wasted mission that ended in one loss.'

The men of 3./KG 30, based at Westerland and Ludwigslust, saw the Wunderbomber in a different light to Göring at this time. The unit Chronik records;

'Technical problems are the order of the day. The snowy winter makes things especially difficult since the Ju 88s are kept out in the open, causing numerous short circuits in the electrical systems, as well as faults in the hydraulics and the engines. We have 16 machines, but the factory still needs to make changes.'

On 26 March, the Staffel's aircraft were prepared for another strike at Scapa Flow. A gunner aboard the Ju 88 of Oberleutnant Helgo Magnussen left the following account;

'This mission was of special significance, since the Home Fleet at Scapa Flow was to be attacked in a large-scale raid for the first time. We also wanted to test the 1800-kg high explosive anti-armour bomb. The *Staffelkapitän*, Hauptmann Arved Crüger and Oberleutnant Magnussen, with whom I flew as a gunner on this mission, had these monstrosities slung under their aircraft.

'The take-off took place from Marx during the afternoon, since a dusk attack was planned, and we had to cover 900 km over the North Sea. During this long flight the U-Boat song "Because we are sailing against England" was repeatedly sung to ward off fatigue and the nervousness about striking an unknown target. The constant question to our navigator-observer about our present position brought forth the same answer, "You violin oinkers (his favorite expression), with your blabbering, I can't get a proper fix". Judging from the flying time and the position of the sun, we should be near the islands. Soon we knew we had reached the target area. We climbed to attack altitude and as we banked into the bay, the pilot picked the largest ship for his bomb. During the dive, a cloud moved between the bombsight and the target. The target had disappeared. We had to stop the dive, pull up and attempt another attack. During the second dive the observer (using strong naval binoculars) warned that the target was a decoy, an old, broken-down freighter. We broke off our attack for the second time. Meanwhile, it had become dark and our aircraft had become caught in the searchlight beams during the pull-up.

'Only after a few desperate manoeuvres was our pilot able to escape the beams. He always had to consider the heavy bomb during these manoeuvres. It was too late for a third attack. If no suitable target was to be found then the bomb was to be brought back, but for that we did not have enough fuel remaining. Our secondary target was an airfield, and we dropped the bomb from an altitude of about 300 m in a glide.

'We were already homebound, when I noticed a light behind us that seemed to be getting larger, and soon the outline of a twin-engined aircraft was noticeable. Strangely, the cockpit of this aircraft was illuminated. We now had to guess whether it was friendly or enemy. Then I noticed the blue flames of the exhausts and we have flame dampers on our aircraft. With this consideration in mind I opened fire. Simultaneously with my burst, a burst of tracer whizzed by my gun position. I discovered the holes in the fairings of the bomb rack after we landed. The enemy aircraft dived away and disappeared. We believed that we had hit the aircraft and we were rid of him, when the next attack came from above. A well-aimed burst

Before becoming one of the most successful Ju 88 pilots and unit leaders in the Mediterranean with I. and II./LG 1, Joachim Helbig flew extensively in the Western campaign in 1940 and mounted 80 sorties against England. He was awarded the Knight's Cross on 24 November 1940, by which time he had sunk 22,000 GRT of enemy shipping. He is seen here at far right in the cockpit of his Ju 88 at Eleusis, in Greece, in August 1941. Helbig's radio operator, Oberfeldwebel Schlund, seen at rear, also wears the Knight's Cross. Note that both Helbig and his observer, Major Stefan (left), are wearing throat microphones, while Unteroffizier Czirpka, as gunner, appears to have squeezed a steel helmet under his flying helmet from the radio operator using the upper machine gun is able to defeat this attack. After these unforeseen attacks, I turn into a lynx looking for prey until my eyes hurt.

'Soon, I see another light on the horizon, a flickering light. I opened fire. It could not have been one of ours since we have been flying on low throttle and must surely be the last ones back. The light continued flickering and did not change position, and we finally figured out that I had been shooting at a star. The laughter that followed cleared away some of the tension that had built up during this mission. On our return flight we had drifted to the south and reached the Dutch coast instead of Westerland. Our radio operator now received a signal from a ground station, and after 9 hours and 20 minutes flying time we landed in Oldenburg. As the aircraft rolled to the revetment the "empty" [fuel] warning light came on.'

In February 1940, two more units began to take delivery of, and convert to, the Ju 88. It was a slow process. The II.(*Kampf*) and III.(*Kampf*) *Gruppen* of *Lehrgeschwader* 1 were based at Langenhagen and Wunstorf/Ludwigslust, respectively. LG 1 had been formed in November 1938 from the *Lehrgeschwader 'Greifswald'* and elements of KG 152, and was intended to function as an operational trials and evaluation unit for new combat aircraft. Its *Stab*, I. II. and III. *Gruppen* were originally equipped with the He 111 and a small number of Bf 109s and Bf 110s, while a IV.(*Stuka*) *Gruppe* operated the Ju 87 and a V.(*Zerstörer*) *Gruppe* was equipped with Bf 110s.

In early 1940, Joachim Helbig was a Leutnant with II./LG 1, and he remembered the conversion process to the Ju 88;

'On the one hand, there were too few training crews available with experience on this new type, which is why, in the time available, only three crews per *Staffel* were retrained on the Ju 88A-1, being instructed on the flight-handling of the bird. On the other hand, flying the Ju 88, which had been designed as a dive-bomber, by a crew previously deployed on the He 111 required a change in aeronautical and weapons functions – at least those for elements affecting the pilot and the observer.'

Regardless of any concerns felt by their crews, KG 30 and LG 1 were deployed against Norway in *Fall Weserübung* as part of Generalleutnant Hans Geisler's X. *Fliegerkorps*. On 9 April, as *Weserübung* operations commenced, aerial reconnaissance by Ju 88s of 1.(F)/122 reported the British Home Fleet 200 km west of Bergen. A force of 47 Ju 88s from all three *Gruppen* of KG 30 and 41 He 111s from I. and II./KG 26 went to attack. The Heinkels made horizontal bombing runs, while the Ju 88s dive-bombed. They sank the destroyer HMS *Gurkha*, seriously damaged the cruisers HMS *Devonshire*, HMS *Glasgow* and HMS *Southampton* and lightly damaged the battleship *Rodney*.

On 15 April, Ju 88s from II. and III./LG 1 entered the fray, flying armed reconnaissance over the Haröy, Molde and Lang fjords as well as bombing sorties against suspected enemy radio transmitting stations, similar missions continuing for the rest of the month. In the late afternoon of the 24th, a Ju 88 from III./LG 1 dropped an SC-250 bomb on an enemy naval vessel in Romsdal Fjord.

One week earlier, on 17 April, the cruiser HMS *Suffolk* was damaged by bombs dropped from a Ju 88A-1 of 6./KG 30 flown by Feldwebel Willi

Schultz. Schultz was already an experienced bomber pilot, having flown missions in Poland and, in the Ju 88, against industrial targets in the Shetlands and along the north coast of Britain, as well as severely damaging a freighter off Newcastle. *Suffolk*, which had been bombarding Stavanger airfield that day, managed to limp back to Scapa Flow on the 18th 'with her quarter-deck awash', having been subjected to seven hours of continuous bombing from the air as it withdrew. Of the 33 attacks endured by *Suffolk*, the most successful were those made in dives by the Ju 88, as opposed to high-level attacks by He 111s. Later, on 18 May, Schultz inflicted similar damage to the battleship HMS *Resolution* off Narvik, and it too was forced to head back to Scapa.

A Ju 88 of KG 30 makes its landing approach towards a timber runway in Norway in early 1940. A lack of Ju 88s at this time meant that the unit was the only *Kampfgeschwader* to operate the type in the Norwegian campaign

For such a record, Willi Schultz was decorated with the Knight's Cross on 19 June, becoming one of the first *Kampfflieger* to receive the award. During the autumn of 1940, he would go on to fly day and night missions against industrial targets and ports in the south of England until he failed to return to base on the night of 19/20 November. It is believed his Ju 88A-5 was lost to mechanical trouble rather than engagement by the enemy.

Also awarded the Knight's Cross the same day as Schultz was 28-year-old Kiel-born Oberleutnant Franz Wieting of 6./KG 30. A former member of the personal staff of *General der Flieger* Hugo Sperrle, he volunteered for combat operations and saw action during the Polish campaign. Wieting became one of the relatively small number of KG 30 pilots to conduct operations against British warships in the North Sea in late 1939/early 1940, and when involved in the Norwegian campaign, he was credited with damaging a heavy cruiser west of Namsos, as well as carrying out several low-level bombing and strafing attacks on British positions ashore. Like Schultz, Wieting also took part in raids on Britain in the autumn of 1940. He was killed when his Ju 88A-5 crashed into mountains on the Bulgarian-Serbian border while on a courier flight on 29 June 1941. Wieting is believed to have flown in excess of 100 combat missions prior to his death.

On 19 April 1940 Hitler personally ordered that *Luftflotte* 5 make air attacks against enemy landings at Namsos and Åndalsnes. Leutnant Werner Baumbach of 5./KG 30 was ordered north to the Åndalsnes area, where, flying a Ju 88A-1, he sank the French light cruiser *Émile Bertin*, the flagship of Group Z, the *Marine Nationale* squadron supporting Allied operations off Norway. Baumbach described the mission as follows;

'The moment we leave the coast we are wrapped in a dense snow-storm. In another half-hour, our target, reported as a group of enemy warships, must be reached. We get everything ready for the attack. In the last few moments the tension is tremendous. Then we've suddenly arrived,

A beaming Leutnant Werner Baumbach of 5./KG 30 receives the Knight's Cross from fellow officers, possibly at Oldenburg, following his award on 8 May 1940 for his service in the Norwegian campaign. One of the Luftwaffe's most highly decorated bomber pilots, his anti-shipping successes were achieved flying the Ju 88

recognised the target and yelled out as one man – "a battleship!" From now on we do not let the big "tub" out of sight. At first I think it is a battleship myself, it looks so big in the narrow fjord. But when we get close, I clearly recognise the striking and characteristic form of a cruiser. As clouds cover the target at the same moment I cannot deliver my attack, but have to turn and run in again.'

As dense anti-aircraft fire blasted upwards from the vessels below, Baumbach observed through a break in the clouds how the bombs dropped from other Ju 88s in his formation were falling near, but short of their targets. With the weather deteriorating, Baumbach knew that success on his second run would be essential;

'We are running in. The cruiser tries to escape by zigzagging, but this time we surprise it by appearing through a tiny gap in the clouds. We rush down. Bombs away. The aircraft gives a heave of relief when it has got rid of them. At the same moment my gunner shouts, "Hit mid-ships to starboard!" I step on it and the jagged mountain tops come nearer. I wrench the aircraft just past them. The gunner feverishly takes photographs. Explosions, smoke and flames have hidden our victim, which a few moments later starts to sink. After a last look around we disappear in the clouds.'

That evening, back at Westerland, Baumbach went to the dining hall to eat;

'As we enter, we are told that in the eight o'clock news there will be a special announcement telling the whole world of our successful attack. For the first time in history a cruiser has been sunk from the air.'

On 8 May, Werner Baumbach was decorated with the Knight's Cross for his service record in the Norwegian campaign. He had joined the Luftwaffe in April 1936 and received officer training at Berlin-Gatow. As a Leutnant at the outbreak of war, Baumbach was serving with 6./LG 1. He flew 14 missions in He 111s during the Polish campaign, and on 9 October 1939 carried out his first sortie against the Royal Navy over the North Sea. In November, he was assigned to Major Friedrich-Karl Knust's *Lehrgruppe* 88 based at Greifswald, where he received training on the Ju 88 at Rechlin. Then, at the beginning of 1940, Baumbach was posted to the newly formed 5./KG 30. As the war progressed he would become one of the Luftwaffe's most renowned and highly decorated bomber pilots, always associated with the Ju 88.

Two days after Baumbach's attack on the *Émile Bertin* on 19 April, Åndalsnes came under attack when the roads leading out of the town, along which Allied troops were making their way having disembarked in the Molde and Romsdals Fjords, were bombed by He 111s and Ju 88s from I./KG 30 and LG 1. Four Junkers from III./LG 1 took off from Schlwesig to attack the radio station at Aalesund, with three of them getting close enough to the target to bomb. One SC-250 fell near the radio building while another came down 20 m from the transmitter mast, almost certainly damaging it.

Flying his *Gruppe*'s only Ju 88, 21 April also saw Oberleutnant Helbig of II./LG 1 embark upon a lone mission from Schleswig to attack ship targets southwest of Trondheim. It proved inconclusive and it took Helbig eight and a half hours to fly through bad weather as far as Aalborg, in Denmark, where he made an interim landing. In making his report by telephone to the *Gruppenkommandeur*, Major Kurt Dobratz, at Schleswig, the young pilot received a sharp rebuke and was told to return to base immediately. He did so, landing at night in pouring rain.

The pilot of a Ju 88A-1 from I./KG 51 leans from the cockpit of his aircraft to call out to ground personnel. Note details such as the pulled-back curtain to the left of the glazed panel immediately aft of the 'beetle's eye' nose, the ring sight and muzzle for the forward-firing MG 15 machine gun, the three-bladed VDM propeller and the fairings for the underwing bomb racks to bottom right (*Author's collection*)

Although Ju 88 operations over Denmark and Norway were comparatively sporadic when set against missions conducted by the He 111, they nevertheless proved that, in the hands of a capable crew, the Junkers could be a formidable and accurate bomber. The aircraft's real baptism of fire was yet to come.

BLITZKRIEG IN THE WEST

By February 1940 the German High Command had finalised its plan for the invasion of France and the Low Countries, to be known as *Fall Gelb* (Case Yellow). The aim was for Generaloberst Wilhelm *Ritter* von Leeb's *Heeresgruppe* C to hold the Franco-German border opposite the Maginot Line while Generaloberst Gerd von Rundstedt's *Heeresgruppe* A made the main attack, with the bulk of the German armour, through the forests of the Ardennes in southern Belgium and Luxembourg. Simultaneously, Generaloberst Fedor von Bock's *Heeresgruppe* B was to mount a secondary advance through northern Belgium and southern Holland to draw the main British and French forces north so that von Rundstedt could hit their flank. Von Rundstedt's ground forces were to be supported by *General der Flieger* Albert Kesselring's *Luftflotte* 2, while von Bock's bomber force was to be provided by *General der Flieger* Hugo Sperrle's *Luftflotte* 3.

As a snapshot, on 30 March 1940, total actual bomber strength available to the Luftwaffe in the West, including Scandinavia (not including dive-bombers) was 1656 machines, of which 1102 were operationally ready. By 10 May, according to German records, the Luftwaffe still had 3824 aircraft available for its Western campaign, of which between 936 and 1120 were bombers. Kesselring's *Luftflotte* 2 had just the IV. *Fliegerkorps* under *General der Flieger* Alfred Keller, based to the north facing Holland

and Belgium, with 326 He 111 and Ju 88s assigned for longer-range missions. The latter were drawn from Major Dr Ernst Bormann's III./LG 1, which was based at Wesendorf. To the south, *General der Flieger* Hugo Sperrle's *Luftflotte* 3 had I., II. and V. *Fliegerkorps*, fielding 741 aircraft comprising the two types, plus the Do 17, all of which were ready for longer-range missions.

In summary, the following Ju 88 *Gruppen* were available for *Fall Gelb*;

IV. *Fliegerkorps*			
III.(K)/LG 1	Major Dr Ernst Bormann	Düsseldorf	12 (5 serviceable)
Stab KG 30	Oberstleutnant Walter Loebel	Oldenburg	2 (2)
I./KG 30	Hauptmann Fritz Doench	Oldenburg	34 (25)
II./KG 30	Hauptmann Claus Kinkelbein	Oldenburg	38 (25)
III./KG 30	Hauptmann Arved Crüger	Marx	30 (20)
Fliegerführer zbV 2			
III./KG 4	Major Wolfgang Neudörffer	Delmenhorst	37 (21)
V. Fliegerkorps			
Stab KG 51	Oberst Josef Kammhuber	Landsberg/Lech	1 (1)
I./KG 51	Major Hans-Bruno Schulz-Heyn	Lechfeld	23 (7)
II./KG 51	Major Friedrich Winkler	München-Riem	39 (29)

III./KG 4, a unit formed from III./KG 253 in May 1939, had begun to take delivery of Ju 88A-1s at Lüneburg in February, which it flew alongside its He 111s. However, unlike the Heinkels, the Junkers did not take part in operations in Scandinavia with this unit, probably because of a lack of adequate training on the type for its crews.

The conversion of *Kampfgeschwader* 51 'Edelweiss' to the Ju 88 was an altogether more wholesale affair. *Stab*, I. and III. *Gruppen* of this *Geschwader* had been established in May 1939 from elements of KG 255, while II. *Gruppe* was newly formed in April 1940. KG 51's mixed-type force of 67 He 111s and 75 Ju 88s was spread across five airfields (posing a challenge to unit communications and logistics), and its serviceability status of 63 per cent for its He 111s and 88.5 per cent for its Ju 88s was considered to be below the Luftwaffe average. The conversion process took longer than expected, with 3. *Staffel* not completing the switch until the end of May.

In reality, the bulk of bombing operations during the *Blitzkrieg* in the West were undertaken by He 111s, although the Ju 88s of I. and II./KG 51 mounted at least 44 sorties in opposition to the evacuation of the British Expeditionary Force (BEF) from the beaches of Dunkirk on 27 May. It was here, when confronted for the first time by determined RAF opposition in the shape of Spitfires that the *Wunderbomber* received a bloody nose.

Flying from Lechfeld, for example, the crew of Leutnant Alfons Berger of 2./KG 51 were still some way from the French coast when they spotted the dense pillars of black smoke spiralling to the sky from the bombed harbour at Dunkirk. Berger approached the port and, together with his observer, selected the ship to be his target. He put his Ju 88A-1 into a dive, but as he did so, the vessel below began to take evasive manoeuvres, escaping Berger's sights. Berger banked away and pulled up, while his gunners covered the sky behind with their MG 15s. Suddenly, a formation of RAF Spitfires approached the Junkers, opening fire. Berger was struck in

the shoulder and one of his gunners was hit in the arm and also wounded in his eyes. The German gunners desperately returned fire, but one weapon suffered a burst barrel. With an engine hit and out of action, Berger turned back to the coast, escorted for some of the way by the British fighters.

Their attempt to bail out was foiled by a jammed canopy jettison lever and they eventually crash-landed in Brussels, the entire crew spending the next few weeks in hospital. of 1./KG 51 and see service flying Ju 88A-4s in Russia, where he was eventually shot down by Soviet fighters and killed on 27 January 1943. He was awarded the *Deutsches Kreuz in Gold* and promoted posthumously to Hauptmann.

LG 1's Ju 88s were also active during the campaign, but conditions proved tough. During the morning of 12 May, 11 Ju 88A-1s of Bormann's III. *Gruppe* from Plantlünne attacked three British vessels in the harbour at Vlissingen. They were bounced by three French fighters and one of the Junkers' crewmembers was wounded.

Later in the month, the *Gruppe*'s Ju 88s were detailed to attack enemy shipping in the Channel ports of Calais and Boulogne. On the 21st, enemy ships and harbour installations at Calais were attacked, but the Junkers tangled with Spitfires and the aircraft of Unteroffizier Richard Tilsner was heavily damaged. Tilsner was able to crash-land his aircraft near Cambrai, but the entire crew suffered wounds. The next day III./LG 1 undertook ground-attack and anti-shipping sorties around Boulogne. It was during these operations that Oberleutnant Karl-Heinz Schomann of 9. *Staffel* managed to inflict four hits on an 8000-ton tanker, which duly sank. It

This Ju 88A-1, probably from III./KG 30, is bombed up at an airfield in Denmark or the Netherlands, the armourers using a hydraulic trolley to raise the weapons to the underwing racks. The aircraft appears to have the yellow spinners of III. *Gruppe* had not been an easy task, for by the time Schomann returned to base on one engine, his Ju 88 had received 140 hits after being attacked by four Spitfires. Schomann later had 20 shell splinters removed from the back of his head and a bullet extricated from his left shoulder. His radio operator had also been badly wounded. Aside from the damaged inflicted by the quartet of RAF fighters, the Ju 88 had also been hit by ground fire on its return flight.

Schomann, who was awarded the Iron Cross First Class for this accomplishment five days later, would recover and return to duty as Technical Officer of III./LG 1 from June 1940. He had entered the Luftwaffe in November 1936, and while with 8.(K)/*Lehrgeschwader* '*Greifswald*' had ferried He 111s to the *Legion Condor* in Spain. Schomann took part in the Polish campaign, as well as operations over Britain in 1940, during which he suffered a similar episode to the one he had experienced over Boulogne, when his Ju 88 was hit by anti-aircraft fire. He was appointed the Technical Officer for the entire *Geschwader* at the beginning of 1941 and then served in the Mediterranean. His career in that theatre is recounted in detail in Chapter 5.

Another Ju 88 pilot to see action over the Channel ports in May 1940 was Oberleutnant Sigmund-Ulrich *Freiherr* von Gravenreuth, who had only joined 1./KG 30 from 3./KG 40 earlier that same month after having fought in Norway. On 20 May, I./KG 30 relocated from Oldenburg to Amsterdam-Schiphol, from where the *Gruppe* carried out attacks on Dunkirk. This day would also mark the beginning of a career that would see von Gravenreuth emerge as an anti-shipping specialist, when he damaged a 16,000-ton vessel in the River Scheldt, which was later sunk by Ju 87s.

Subsequently appointed *Staffelkapitän* of 1./KG 30, von Gravenreuth led his unit so successfully in the Channel and the North Sea that he was awarded the Knight's Cross on 24 November 1940 – by which time he had personally sunk vessels totalling 50,000 Gross Registered Tonnage (GRT), including two troop ships and a destroyer. He would go on to be appointed *Kommodore* of KG 30 in September 1943, but only after von Gravenreuth had suffered the loss of his right leg below the knee as a result of wounds sustained during an anti-shipping mission over the Arctic Ocean.

NEW AIRCRAFT, NEW UNITS, NEW BATTLES

The delay in delivery of Jumo 211F and J engines resulted in the introduction of the interim Ju 88A-5 variant in the spring of 1940 while arrival of the definitive A-4 was awaited. Aside from the extended wing mentioned earlier and powered by 1200 hp Jumo 211Bs, the A-5 featured a strengthened undercarriage intended to take the weight of increased externally-carried 250-kg bombs fitted to ETC racks outboard of the engines. Armament in early A-5s remained essentially the same as later A-1s, with MG 15s in the forward cockpit canopy, two further such weapons in the rear canopy and a single gun in the rear of the ventral gondola. There was also the option to mount machine guns in the glazed nose and on side fittings in the cockpit. The aircraft's radio equipment was improved in the A-5, and incorporated a FuG 25 IFF transceiver.

LUFTFLOTTE 2, Brussels, Belgium, Generalfeldmarschall Albert Kesselring		
Kampfgeschwader 76, Oberstleutnant Frölich		
II. Gruppe	Creil	(28)
Aufklärungsgruppe 122, Hauptmann Bohm		
5. Staffel	Haute-Fontaine	(A small number of Ju 88s)
Kampfgeschwader 4, Oberstleutnant Rath		
III. Gruppe	Amsterdam-Schiphol	(23)
Aufklärungsgruppe 122, Oberstleutnant Koehler		
3. Staffel	Eindhoven	(a small number of Ju 88s)
LUFTFLOTTE 3, Paris, France, Generalfeldmarschall Hugo Sperrle		
Lehrgeschwader 1, Oberst Bülowius		
Stabschwarm	Orléans-Bricy	(1)
I. Gruppe	Orléans-Bricy	(23)
II. Gruppe	Orléans-Bricy	(24)
III. Gruppe	Châteaudun	(23)
Kampfgeschwader 40, Oberstleutnant Geisse		
Stabschwarm	Brest-Guipavas	(1)
Kampfgruppe 806, Major Emig		
–	Nantes and Caen	(22)
Aufklärungsgruppe 121, Hauptmann Kerber		
3. Staffel	North-West France	(6)
Kampfgeschwader 51, Major Schulz-Heyn		
Stabschwarm	Paris-Orly	(1)
I. Gruppe	Melun-Villaroche	(21)
II. Gruppe	Étampes-Montdésir	(24)
III. Gruppe	Étampes-Montdésir	(25)
Kampfgeschwader 54, Oberstleutnant Höhne		
Stabschwarm	Evreux	(0)
I. Gruppe	Evreux	(29)
II. Gruppe	André-de-l'Eure	(23)
Aufklärungsgruppe 121, Hauptmann Kerber		
4. Staffel	Villacoublay	(a small number of Ju 88s)
LUFTFLOTTE 5, Stavanger, Norway, Generaloberst Hans-Jürgen Stumpff		
Kampfgeschwader 30, Oberstleutnant Loebel		
Stabschwarm	Aalborg	(1)
I. Gruppe	Aalborg	(34)
III. Gruppe	Aalborg	(27)
Aufklärungsgruppe Ob. d. L., Oberstleutnant Rowehl		
1. Staffel	Various	(a small number of Ju 88s)

The A-5 proved popular with crews as a result of improved control response, although there was no increase in performance over the A-1. Deliveries began to reach frontline units just as the Luftwaffe's next big campaign loomed.

With much of western Europe now under German occupation and the BEF kicked out of France from the beaches at Dunkirk, Adolf Hitler looked – perhaps reluctantly – to eliminate the threat posed by Great Britain to his continued war aims. To conquer Britain, however, would require a strong, sustained air campaign followed by an amphibious invasion. Werner Baumbach of KG 30 once admitted to his fellow Ju 88 pilots in 1940, 'We know that England is the hardest nut to be cracked in this war'.

At the beginning of July, the Luftwaffe could field 4074 frontline aircraft (excluding transports) against the RAF's 1963. Within this figure were

1380 bombers (He 111s, Ju 88s and Do 17s, including those flown by units in Scandinavia and northern Germany, but excluding dive-bombers), although actual serviceability is not known, and some sources state that it was less than 50 per cent in July.

For the campaign against Britain, the Luftwaffe would continue to be marshalled by the *Luftflotten* that were deployed in *Fall Gelb*. The component units formed what was essentially a daylight operational force which, apart from minelaying, undertook very limited night activity. The bulk of the bomber force was comprised of He 111-equipped units, but in the Do 17 and Ju 88 the Heinkel had fast and flexible competitors. Unlike the He 111, which had been designed and built as both a transport and bomber, the Ju 88 had been created as a thoroughbred '*Schnellbomber*'.

The Order of Battle opposite, dated 1 August 1940, shows an increasing number of Ju 88 units, which included the newly equipped II./KG 76, KGr.806 and I. and II./KG 54, as well as a small number of reconnaissance *Staffeln* equipped with modified A-1s and A-5s or examples of the new D-0 series, with the rear bomb-bay adapted for camera fitment.

For the German bomber crews, the air campaign against England in 1940 broke down into two distinct phases – first, the daylight bombing period from July to September and, secondly, the night-bombing phase from September into the late spring of 1941. The first of these two phases constituted essentially a hard slogging match against the RAF, with bombers battling to get across the Channel, then penetrating the British defensive fighter screen over southern England, quite often without escort, and attempting to reach their targets. Once that had been accomplished, they had to make it back to their landing grounds on the Continent, invariably running the gauntlet of RAF fighters once again. For the *Kampfflieger*, unlike their fighter comrades, operations over England were much less free, just as dangerous and much less glamorous. As Dieter Lukesch, latterly a Knight's Cross-holder with Ju 88-equipped KG 76, remarked, 'Bombing was a dirty business'.

Operations started in early July with initial armed reconnaissance missions and probing raids by Ju 88s across the English Channel against coastal targets. These would involve either single aircraft or small formations flying, in reality, *Störangriffe* (nuisance raids) against merchant shipping, ports and harbours, and those inland industrial locations within range, preferably with the aid of cloud cover. On 20 July, Ju 88s undertook minelaying operations off the east coast, as well as around the Isle of Wight – a form of low-level, low-speed operations that required extremely accurate navigation.

Elsewhere that day, Major Hans Emig's *Kampfgruppe* 806, equipped with 27 Ju 88s of which 18 were serviceable, began 'armed sea reconnaissance' missions and attacks on enemy shipping with both guns and bombs. The *Gruppe*'s operational area lay to the west of England, over the St George's Channel and the Irish Sea, while small raids were also mounted against the towns and ports of Pembroke, Cardiff, Newport and Liverpool.

But it would not be until August that Ju 88s were despatched in numbers against Britain. At 0930 hrs on the 11th, 38 Ju 88s of I. and II./KG 54, led by Major Otto Höhne and Major Kurt Leonhardy respectively, took off from Evreux and St André to attack harbour installations, fuel storage tanks, a weapons depot and ships moored within Portland harbour and in the nearby Dorset port town of Weymouth. The raid was augmented by 20 He 111s from KG 27, and the whole German force was escorted by 91 Bf 110s from ZG 2 and 30 Bf 109s from JG 2.

The raid was detected forming up off and over the Cherbourg Peninsula by the British radar station at Ventnor, so that by the time it was nearing the British coast across a front eight kilometres wide, RAF Spitfires and Hurricanes had been scrambled. Amidst a huge aerial encounter over Weymouth Bay between the German and British fighters, the Heinkels doggedly carried out their horizontal bombing, while the Ju 88s attacked specific targets using diving attacks, striking the oil storage farm within Portland naval base and setting two tanks on fire. Upon their return, the Ju 88s reported hits on oil tanks and wharves, as well as setting fire to several buildings and hitting two freighters each of around 4000 tons.

However, there had been a high cost to pay for this success. Five Ju 88s were lost, including the *Führungsmaschine* (lead aircraft) flown by Oberleutnant Hans Schott of the *Stab* II./KG 54 that was carrying the *Gruppenkommandeur*, Major Leonhardy. An experienced officer who had received flying training at the covert German base at Lipetsk, in western Russia, in the early 1930s, Leonhardy had subsequently become a commercial pilot with Deutsche Lufthansa. He later attended the *Luftskriegakademie* at Berlin-Gatow and was a recipient of an advanced flying certificate.

KG 54 struck again on 13 August (*Adler Tag* – Eagle Day), which was the date that regular bombing operations commenced in force against targets on the British mainland; primarily airfields and associated installations, the supply network, the aircraft industry and centres of anti-aircraft artillery production. The plan was to overwhelm, exhaust and eliminate the British defence by sheer might ahead of a German invasion. For this task, *Luftflotten* 2 and 3 were firstly to secure air superiority over southern England by operating against enemy aircraft, especially those of RAF Fighter Command, in the air and on the ground, then to attack the aforementioned targets, while *Luftflotte* 5 was to divert and pin down British defence forces in the north by attacks 'on airfields in the Newcastle area'. It was hoped that the whole offensive would require no more than four days to smash Fighter Command in southern England and its support infrastructure. After that had been accomplished, the attack was to roll northwards beyond a tactical line from Kings Lynn to Leicester, advancing sector by sector until the whole of England was covered by daylight bombardment.

KG 54's targets on the 13th were the airfield at Odiham and the Royal Aeronautical Establishment's base at Farnborough. A total of 20 Ju 88s from II. *Gruppe*, now under the command of Leonhardy's successor, Hauptmann Karl-Bernhard Schlaeger, took off at 0555 hrs for Odiham and arrived to drop 35 SC-250s, four incendiaries and 52 SC-50s, of which 13 had delayed fuses. The crews reported hits on hangars and nearby buildings. The 18 Ju 88s of I./KG 54 arrived at Farnborough at 0748 hrs and dropped 64 SC-50 bombs, of which half were fitted with delayed fuses, as well as four SC-250s and two 250-kg incendiary bombs. The crews reported a good dispersal of their bombs. The Ju 88s ran into

Leutnant Werner Baumbach (second from left) poses with his crew – bombardier, radio operator and gunner – in front of their blacked-out Ju 88A-5, possibly at Gilze-Rijen in late 1940 during the height of the night *Blitz*. Note that even the '*Adler*' *Geschwader*'s diving eagle emblem has been toned down for nocturnal operations

fierce opposition from RAF Hurricanes from the moment they crossed the British coast. Two aircraft were lost from the *Stab* of I./KG 54, while four from II. *Gruppe* were also downed, with others damaged.

During the campaign over England in 1940, as far as the Ju 88 crews were concerned, it was their speed that saved them from suffering the weight of losses felt by the Heinkel and Dornier units.

The campaign raged on with bitter intensity throughout August, during which night raids commenced. At this stage a paradox crept in. The losses in all bomber types suffered in the six-week period from mid-July to the end of August due to the stubbornness and effectiveness of the British defence forced a review of Luftwaffe strategy. Göring and most of his senior commanders believed, as a result of their (flawed) air intelligence, that Fighter Command was defeated. The Luftwaffe thus began to escalate its attacks, broadly in keeping with original intentions, moving progressively inland to encompass production facilities and the RAF sector airfields. However, the eventual switch from the sector airfields to attacks on London was a deliberate move based on the assumption that Fighter Command – or what was left of it – would have to get airborne in strength to defend a target of such importance.

On 2 September Göring ordered that London should become the subject of continuous raids, aimed at specific targets, with the objective of reducing military capability and weakening the will to resist. Thus began the war against Britain's cities and their civilian populations. So the relatively few *Gruppen* of Ju 88 *Schnellbombers* – III./KG 4, KG 51,

I. and II./KG 54 and II./KG 76, along with the recently added contribution of KG 77, which had also converted to the Ju 88 during the summer – were deployed as horizontal bombers during the *Blitz*. In this, they suffered, particularly KG 77, whose losses in two raids in September 1940 accounted for 40 per cent of the month's Ju 88 casualties. In a raid on London docks on the 18th, the *Gruppenkommandeur* of III./KG 77, Major Maxim Kless, was lost when his Ju 88A-1 was shot down over north Kent by Spitfires. Like Leonhardy of KG 54, Kless was another veteran of covert training in Soviet Russia during the 1930s and a graduate of the *Luftskriegakademie* at Gatow, speaking Russian and Japanese fluently.

The Knight's Crosses given to Ju 88 pilots during the Battle of Britain were predominantly for operations against shipping. Berliner Walter Loebel joined the Luftwaffe in July 1935 and enrolled in general staff training prior to the outbreak of war. On 1 April 1939 he took command of I./KG 257, remaining in this position through its redesignation to I./KG 26. On 15 November of that year, with the rank of Oberstleutnant, Loebel was reassigned to take command of the new KG 30. He would fly anti-shipping missions against British targets as an observer, and during his tenure as *Kommodore* in the *Geschwader*'s first months of existence, the unit claimed 663,000 GRT of shipping sunk around the British Isles, with another 528,000 GRT damaged. In May 1940, again under Loebel's leadership, KG 30 carried out successful early strikes against the *Luchtvaartafdeeling* (Royal Netherlands Air Force), preparing the way for German paratroops. For such leadership Loebel was awarded the Knight's Cross on 29 July 1940.

In August he was posted to the command staff of Kesselring's *Luftflotte* 2 and later saw service in Russia where, on 6 September 1941, his Ju 88A-1 failed to return from a reconnaissance mission over Smolensk.

Another recipient from KG 30 was Feldwebel Otto Eichloff, who had joined the 4. *Staffel* of the *'Adler' Geschwader* from 8./KG 51. One of the Westerland-based crews, he was involved in the sinking of two enemy cruisers off Norway in April 1940, one of them possibly *Suffolk*, as well as a 4000-ton freighter. For his actions Eichloff was awarded both the Iron Cross First and Second Classes on the same day on 3 May, before taking part in the campaign in the West. Having sunk a transport on the Maas Estuary and bombed enemy ground installations during the *Blitzkrieg*, he then embarked on raids against Britain in the summer. Eichloff was awarded the Knight's Cross on 16 August 1940.

At 38, Major Erich Bloedorn, the *Kommandeur* of III./KG 4 would have been considered 'old' to have won the Knight's Cross when he became a recipient on 13 October 1940 for his leadership of the *Gruppe* during early operations over the Channel in the campaign against England. In the early 1930s, Bloedorn had spent time in China as a military advisor

Hans-Joachim 'Hajo' Herrmann, photographed shortly after his promotion to Hauptmann in December 1940, commenced flying the Ju 88 operationally over Norway during that year, before carrying out many missions in the Junkers bombers over Britain. A veteran aviator of the Spanish Civil War, he would go on to become one of the Luftwaffe's most decorated bomber pilots. After the campaign against England, he flew with KG 30 in attacks against Allied convoys in the Mediterranean and on the Polar Sea Front. In the latter part of the war, he was a principal architect of *Wilde Sau* nightfighting, was appointed to command the 1. *Jagddivision* and 9. *Fliegerdivision* and, in 1945, also became involved in the creation of a controversial air-ramming command, *Sonderkommando Elbe*. Herrmann flew 320 combat missions, including 50 in Spain and 30 in single-seat nightfighters. He was awarded the Swords to the Knight's Cross with Oak Leaves on 23 August 1943 and ended the war with the rank of Oberst in a civilian capacity. He returned to Germany in 1936 and joined the Luftwaffe. Appointed *Staffelkapitän* of 7./KG 4 on 1 January 1940, he took part in operations over Norway and in the West, where he carried out attacks on enemy airfields and troop concentrations and made flights over Dunkirk. On 19 May Bloedorn was wounded when his Ju 88A-1 was shot down by British fighters between Ostend and Boulogne.

After recovery, and having been promoted to the rank of Major, he took command of III. *Gruppe* and led the unit with great success, accounting for the sinking of three destroyers and 2000 tons of merchant shipping. On 16 October 1940, three days after being decorated with the Knight's Cross, Bloedorn was appointed *Kommodore* of KG 30 as the replacement for Walter Loebel.

Decorated the same day as Bloedorn was Oberleutnant Hajo Herrmann, who would enjoy a glittering Luftwaffe service career. The 27-year-old Herrmann had first put on a uniform when he became a policeman in Hamburg in 1933, and he joined the Luftwaffe two years later. Herrmann served as a bomber pilot in the *Legion Condor* during the Spanish Civil War, where he flew 50 missions, and then returned to the Reich to join 7./KG 4 and serve alongside Bloedorn. He flew the He 111 over Poland, before quickly converting to the Ju 88 for operations over Norway and the West. Herrmann's aircraft was shot down over the beaches of Dunkirk on 31 May 1940, although he landed in German-occupied territory. Like Bloedorn, he was appointed to lead 7./KG 4 and flew many missions against Britain until a crash-landing at Amsterdam-Schiphol on 19 October 1940 hospitalised him for six weeks. Herrmann, who had been awarded the Knight's Cross a week before the accident, was promoted to the rank of Hauptmann shortly thereafter.

Luftwaffe bomber operations against Britain, the Royal Navy and mercantile tonnage continued doggedly into late 1940, but as the autumn turned into winter, by December, rain, snow, fog, ice and thick cloud had hampered flying so much that hardly any raids were flown. In the Reich, however, Adolf Hitler and his military planners were casting their eyes to the south and the east, where there would be new battles in which the Ju 88 would play a leading role and its profile would become much higher.

CHAPTER TWO

LONG-RANGE NIGHT INTRUDERS

ike the V5, the seventh prototype (appropriately designated the V7) of the Ju 88 to be built at Junkers Dessau had the customary glazed nose replaced by a solid, unglazed nose-cap intended for the testing of fixed, forward-firing guns, the aim being to assess the aircraft as a heavy fighter, or *Zerstörer*, for what would become the C series. Initial experiments conducted during the autumn of 1938 had involved the installation of three machine guns and a cannon intended to fire through the usual glazed design, but eventually this was abandoned in favour of a solid structure, as well as the removal of the aircraft's ventral gondola. In this configuration, tests proved that the Ju 88, powered by either BMW or Jumo 211A engines, was a stable gun platform, as did further *Zerstörer* trials conducted in 1940 with two more prototypes, the V15 and V19, at the weapons testing establishment at Tarnewitz.

Production of the Ju 88C commenced in 1939, with a small quantity of pre-production C-0s converted from existing A-1s for operational trials, before the first C-2s were delivered to the *Zerstörerstaffel* KG 30 at Perleberg under Oberleutnant Herbert Bönsch in February 1940. These aircraft, packing a punch with their 20 mm MG FF cannon and three MG 17s mounted to the right of the nose and powered by 1200 hp Jumo 211B-1 engines, had almost three times the range of the then most common *Zerstörer*, the Bf 110. Defensively, the C-2 could count on a single machine gun in the rear of the cockpit and in the rear of the gondola.

An early Ju 88C-6 *Nachtzerstörer* intended for long-range night-intruding and fighting, photographed probably in 1942. The aircraft lacks radar but is armed with a 20 mm MG FF cannon and three MG 81 or MG 131 machine guns in its solid nose, as well as a further machine gun in the forward position in the ventral *Bola*. The Jumo 211J engines have flame-dampers fitted and the 'Englandblitz' emblem of the nightfighter arm adorns the nose. Note that the white surrounds of all national markings have been blacked out, although light blue undersides have been retained

In April, six C-2s were relocated to Stavanger/Sola, in Norway, to join KG 30's A-1s, and they took part in free-range patrols as well as serving as escorts for bombers attacking other Norwegian targets. Very quickly (Z)./KG 30's pilots filed claims for the shooting down of two Wellingtons from No 149 Sqn that had attempted to attack the German battlecruisers *Scharnhorst* and *Gneisenau* and the cruiser *Hipper* off the coast of Norway on 12 April. In a day that saw a series of large-scale battles fought between RAF bombers and aggressively flown single- and twin-engined German fighters, the two Wellingtons fell to Oberfeldwebel Martin Jeschke at 1645 hrs and future nightfighter ace Unteroffizier Peter Lauffs five minutes later – these were the very first aerial victories credited to the Ju 88. Two more Wellingtons were lightly damaged. (Z)./KG 30 in turn lost the Ju 88C-2 flown by Unteroffizier Erwin Maus, his aircraft crashing into the sea southwest of Sola with the loss of the crew. A second Junkers *Zerstörer* crash-landed on Sola airfield, suffering 50 per cent damage.

The following day Lauffs claimed a Hudson destroyed east of Stavanger, although he had in fact only damaged an aircraft from No 230 Sqn that was undertaking a reconnaissance flight along the Norwegian coast in search of German naval vessels. His 'victory' duly remained unconfirmed. The crew of the Hudson in turned stated, erroneously, that they had shot Lauffs' Ju 88C-2 down. Jeschke claimed another Hudson destroyed over Stavanger on 17 April, although again the No 233 Sqn machine escaped destruction. On the 25th the *Zerstörer* shot up a number of Gladiators from No 263 Sqn found on a lake airfield at Lesjaskog while escorting Ju 88As of 2./KG 30 on a mission to the Åndalsnes and Dombås areas. During the strafing runs (Z)./KG 30's Obergefreiter Richard and Bf 110 pilot Leutnant Manfred Riegel from I./ZG 76 claimed four Gladiators destroyed between them.

Five days later, three Ju 88C-2s escorted Junkers bombers from 2./KG 30 on an attack on Setnesmoen landing ground. Leutnant Pack, future long-range nightfighter ace Oberfeldwebel Kurt Hermann and Unteroffizier Alfred Wiemann each destroyed a Norwegian air force Fokker C.V biplane during strafing passes.

Further coastal patrol work and fighter escort for the He 111s of KG 26 continued through May, as well as covering a drop by *Fallschirmjäger* on Björnfell on 16 May. That same day (Z)./KG 30 claimed its final aerial victories of the campaign when Oberleutnant Bönsch and Unteroffizier Lauffs clashed with Fleet Air Arm (FAA) Blackburn Skuas of 803 Naval Air Squadron, embarked in *Ark Royal*. Bönsch was credited with a 'Blackburn Roc' destroyed southeast of Narvik, while Lauffs claimed one or two victories, which he thought were either Rocs or Skuas. One FAA fighter was indeed forced down in Rombaksfjord.

(Z)./KG 30's last combat loss in Norway came on 7 June when a Ju 88C-2 was hit by ground fire while strafing the ore railway line that ran from Sweden into Norway, the *Zerstörer* force landing near Björnfjell. Nine days later the crews from the unit were ordered to Ludwigslust, where they received nightfighter training, before being moved again to Düsseldorf. Here, the unit was redesignated as 4./NJG 1 in early July, still under the command of Bönsch.

This proved to be a timely development. In the summer of 1940, the overall commander of the still fledgling nightfighter force as head of

1. *Nachtjagddivision*, Oberst Josef Kammhuber (formerly *Kommodore* of KG 51) decided that he would adopt a policy of 'offensive defence' by sending out his fighters to harass RAF Bomber Command formations and airfields. For this he needed heavily armed fighters with range – *Fernnachtjäger* – and thus the Ju 88C fitted his requirement.

Simultaneously, 4./NJG 1 was bolstered by 5./NJG 1, formed from the Bf 110-equipped 1./NJG 1 but equipped with Do 17s, together with a new 6./NJG 1 led by Hauptmann Karl Theodor Hülshoff, who had come from the bomber unit 7./KG 54. The new combined II. *Gruppe* would operate the Ju 88C under the command of *Legion Condor* veteran Major Karl-Heinrich Heyse, but it was not long after establishment that it was relocated on 1 September to Gilze-Rijen, in southern Holland, and then redesignated again, as I./NJG 2, remaining at the same base under Heyse.

In the autumn of 1940, with limited numbers of aircraft available – never more than 20 Ju 88C-2s at any one time – the *Gruppe* began to devise tactics for nocturnal combat operations. After considering options, it was decided the most effective form of attack for the *Fernnachtjäger* would be to infiltrate the RAF bomber streams as they returned to their illuminated home bases, their crews tired after a long mission and thus at their most vulnerable.

Among the earliest proponents of this form of nightfighting was Oberleutnant Kurt Herrmann who, during the evening of 24 October 1940, attacked a Blenheim belonging to No 17 Operational Training Unit (OTU) while it was on a flight over Norfolk. The British bomber managed to land safely despite a burning fuel tank and damage to its hydraulics. A few minutes later, Herrmann attacked what he thought was a Beaufort but which was actually another Blenheim, and although this aircraft also managed to evade being shot down, Herrmann's actions demonstrated what could be achieved by roaming into and over enemy territory. Over the next four months he would go on to claim (inaccurately) seven more enemy aircraft, becoming the 'highest-scoring' nightfighter pilot of the period.

During the clear evening of 10 March 1941, however, Herrmann was on a sortie over eastern England when the right engine of his all-black, bomb-carrying Ju 88C-2 was hit by anti-aircraft fire. Despite jettisoning the ordnance, Herrmann was forced to land near Kings Lynn shortly after midnight and he and his crew were captured by a British Home Guard unit. He would subsequently be awarded the *Deutsches Kreuz in Gold*.

On the same night that Herrmann had attacked the aircraft from the OTU, fellow future *Fernnachtjäger* ace Feldwebel Hans Hahn of 3./NJG 2 had claimed his first victory when he shot down a Whitley of No 102 Sqn (although it was claimed as a Wellington) just after 2300 hrs near Linton-on-Ouse. Hahn would not score again until the night of 2/3 January 1941, when he shot down another No 102 Sqn Whitley over the North Sea, 50 km east of Withernsea, from a force of 47 that had been sent to bomb Bremen.

Hahn was born in Rheydt on 9 February 1919 and had initially trained as a bomber pilot. Indeed, he is believed to have sunk a 4000-GRT freighter off Dunkirk in May 1940. He volunteered for the new nightfighter arm in July 1940. After completion of his night training, Hahn was assigned to 3./NJG 2 and soon credited with his first victory. He was something of

After a six-year service career that had commenced flying coastal patrol aircraft at the outbreak of war, transitioning through the Bf 109, then on to the Ju 88, and with hundreds of missions to his name, Major Paul Semrau was killed on 8 February 1945 when his aircraft was attacked by a Spitfire of No 402 Sqn while landing at Twente airfield in the Netherlands. One of the most successful early night intruder pilots, Semrau was credited with nine victories scored in such operations

The *Fernnachtjäger* lost one of its leading proponents when Leutnant Hans Hahn of I./NJG 2 was killed over England on the night of 11/12 October 1941, his Ju 88C-4 having collided with a British aircraft. Awarded the Knight's Cross on 9 July 1941, he is credited with 12 night victories

The right side of Ju 88C-4 Wk-Nr 360219 at the time it was flown by Oberfeldwebel Wilhelm Beier of 7./NJG 2 and marked with 22 victory bars. His latest kill had been for a 'Manchester', but recent post-war research has revealed that it was in fact a Wellington of No 75 'New Zealand' Sqn that was shot down over the Netherlands in the early hours of 29 August 1942

Leutnant Heinz Strüning, seen here after the award of the Knight's Cross on 29 October 1942, was one of the early *Fernnachtjäger* aces. A former *Zerstörer* pilot, he had claimed nine victories by the end of 1941, some scored during intruder operations

a daredevil, fearless in his intruder missions, but frequently returning to Gilze-Rijen with battle damage or flying on a single engine. On one occasion his Ju 88 returned with a balloon cable wrapped around a wing, which was subsequently removed and used as a trophy in the *Gruppe* mess.

His score surpassed that of Kurt Herrmann when he shot down a Hurricane from No 257 Sqn over Cambridgeshire in the early hours of the morning of 5 May for his tenth victory. None of this was without its toll on the young pilot, however, and both he and his crew were ordered on a month's recuperative leave in the mountains of Lower Silesia. A bright spot came when he was awarded the Knight's Cross on 9 July 1941 for achieving 11 night victories, making him the first recipient in the *Nachtjagd*, along with promotion to leutnant.

By August he had returned to operations, and on the night of the 16/17 he shot down a Wellington of No 104 Sqn over Scunthorpe while on its way to bomb Köln. Yet again, wreckage from the British bomber struck Hahn's Ju 88 and he returned to the Netherlands on one engine. On the night of 11/12 October, Hahn's Ju 88C-4 collided with a twin-engined Oxford training aircraft of No 12 Flying Training School near the blacked-out town of Grantham, in Lincolnshire, during an intruder mission over England involving five aircraft from I./NJG 2. The remains of both Hahn and his crew were found burnt out in the wreckage of their aircraft at Barrowby, also in Lincolnshire. The last I./NJG 2 heard from Hahn was a radio message at 2045 hrs, but by the following morning his comrades at Gilze-Rijen had accepted that he would not be returning. Hahn is credited with 13 night victories.

It is possible that fellow ace Feldwebel Heinz Strüning of 1./NJG 2 scored his first victory during the early evening of 23 November 1940, when he lodged a claim for a Wellington shot down over the North Sea 50 km west of Scheveningen. However, it is equally possible this aircraft (from No 214 Sqn) may have been shot down by his *Gruppe* comrades Hauptmann Karl Theodor Hülshoff of 3. *Staffel* or Leutnant Kurt Herrmann (who claimed a Hampden) for his sixth victory. Whatever the case, Strüning would go on to enjoy an impressive operational record that started with 66 intruder sorties over England and culminated in 250 night missions, from which he would be credited with 56 victories by December 1944.

Born on 13 January 1912 in Neviges in the Rheinland, Strüning first saw service in August 1939 with 5./ZG 26 as a *Zerstörer* pilot, prior to transferring to (Z)./KG 30 on 11 April 1940, with whom he flew sorties over Norway, including Narvik. He was later assigned to nightfighter training and joined I./NJG 2 for *Fernnachtjäger* operations. By the end of 1941 he was credited with nine victories, numbering him amongst the most successful intruder pilots. Strüning transferred to 3./NJG 1 and then 9./NJG 1, where he was appointed *Staffelkapitän*. Awarded the Knight's

Cross on 29 October 1942 for 23 nocturnal kills and then the *Eichenlaub* (Oak Leaves) on 20 July 1944 for his 50th victory, Strüning survived until 24 December 1944, when his Bf 110 was attacked by an RAF Mosquito intruder near Wesendorf. He attempted to bail out, but struck the tail unit of his aircraft and was killed.

The *Fernnachtjäger* became a thorn in the side of the RAF in eastern England in 1941, for aside from engagements in the air, the Ju 88s were also attacking the British infrastructure. Four nights after Herrmann was captured on 10/11 March, Junkers intruders attacked Wittering airfield in Cambridgeshire, dropping six bombs that killed five personnel and injured a further 15. A hangar was hit, as well as the officers' mess, a cinema and offices, and five aircraft were destroyed on the ground, including three Beaufighters. Such attacks would become a regular occurrence.

Another pilot to become an early nightfighter ace through intruder missions in the Ju 88 was Oberleutnant Paul Semrau, the *Staffelkapitän* of 3./NJG 2. In the predawn hours of 11 February 1941 he had accounted for his first kills – two No 21 Sqn Blenheims shot down within the space of five minutes over Feltwell airfield, the second of which he attacked as it made its landing approach. The bomber caught fire as it came to a halt on the ground, with only its gunner managing to escape the aircraft alive.

Prussian by birth, Semrau's first operational posting at the outbreak of war was with 3./Kü.Fl.Gr.106, before moving to 2./ZG 2, where he flew the Bf 109D as a *Staffelkapitän* until March 1940. He was then assigned to (Z)./KG 30, where he transitioned to the Ju 88 before becoming a nightfighter pilot from July 1940. In the early hours of 18 July 1941 he shot down a Wellington (which he claimed was a Blenheim) from No 305 Sqn near Digby in Lincolnshire, as it returned from a raid to Rotterdam. It was his eighth victory. By 21 September 1941 he had chalked up nine

Groundcrew assembled for a photograph around the left side of Ju 88C-4 Wk-Nr 360219 of 4./NJG 2 prior to it being transferred to 10./NJG 1. This aircraft was at one time flown by Oberfeldwebel Wilhelm Beier, and its tail assembly is adorned with his 36 claimed victories and a depiction of the Knight's Cross that was awarded to him on 11 October 1941, when his tally stood at 14 kills. On the night of 15/16 October 1942, Beier claimed the shooting down of a B-24, two Stirlings and a 'Manchester', although only the latter can be accounted for by the loss of a No 57 Sqn Lancaster over the North Sea

Oberfeldwebel Wilhelm Beier (centre) receives the Knight's Cross from Generalleutnant Josef Kammhuber, commander of the XII. *Fliegerkorps*, at Gilze-Rijen in October 1941

Ju 88C-4 R4+GM, flown by Oberfeldwebel Wilhelm Beier of III./NJG 2, is seen at Gilze-Rijen after a taxiing accident in which the aircraft's radar antennae were sheared off and its propellers destroyed. None of Beier's claims appear to have been applied to the tail assembly of this machine, which has been finished in the standard daylight RLM 70/71 splinter pattern on its uppersurfaces

nocturnal kills, making him one of the most successful *Fernnachtjäger* before he was transferred to the Mediterranean.

The following month, on the 11th, Oberfeldwebel Wilhelm Beier was decorated with the Knight's Cross in recognition of having achieved 14 night intruder victories. A native of Homberg in the Niederrhein, Beier had first lodged a victory claim while flying a Ju 88C-2 of 3./NJG 2 on 16/17 December 1940, his victim reportedly being a Hurricane. Beier preferred to stalk his quarry over the North Sea rather than penetrate beyond the British coast, although on one occasion, on the night of 7/8 May, he *claimed* a Wellington over the Norfolk coastal town of Wells-next-the Sea. The author has emphasised the word 'claimed', since the majority of Beier's eventual 36 victories cannot be matched against RAF losses. Beier would go on to see action with both NJGs 1 and 3 and also serve as an instructor with the *Ausbildungskommando Ost* (Eastern Training Command), before ending his war training to fly the Me 262B-1a jet nightfighter.

Also operational on the night of 7/8 May 1941 was another member of 3. *Staffel*, future ace Unteroffizier Alfons Köster. Twenty-two-year-old Köster was the son of a forester from Hüingsen in Westphalia. One of ten siblings, he had scored his first aerial victory on 9 April 1941 when he shot down a Hurricane (which he claimed as a Defiant) of No 257 Sqn over East Anglia. Subsequently, he flew regular sorties to England, and on 3 October he was credited with his 11th and final *Fernnachtjäger* victory when he shot down a Stirling of No 7 Sqn as it returned to Oakington airfield in Cambridgeshire.

Köster had been attracted by the airfield flare path, and the Stirling had flown directly in front of his Ju 88 with all its lights on as the bomber flew over Oakington. A witness on the ground recalled how the Junkers nightfighter pursued the Stirling, 'firing bursts every few seconds'. After some minutes of evasive flying and pursuit, another Stirling arrived on the scene and began to chase the German intruder. The three aircraft began to circle, but eventually Köster managed to fire an accurate burst and the British bomber erupted into flames. Although two crew bailed out, the remainder went down with their aircraft, which crashed near Caxton Gibbet. Köster then flew northwest (*text continues on page 49*)

COLOUR PLATES

1
Ju 88A-1 Wk-Nr 299 9K+HS of III./KG 51, Etampes-Mondésir, France, summer 1940

2
Ju 88A-1 4D+CR of 1./KG 30, Oldenburg, Germany, May 1940

3
Ju 88A-4 B3+BM of 4./KG 54, Saint-André-de-l'Eure, France, August 1940

4
Ju 88A-5 Wk-Nr 4219 of an unknown *Staffel* from KG 30, possibly Gilze–Rijen, the Netherlands, late 1940/early 1941

5
Ju 88A-5 L1+GH flown by Oberfeldwebel Otto Leupert, I./LG 1, Benghazi-Benina, Libya, October 1941

6
Ju 88A-5 F1+JR of 7./KG 76, Rakopolje, Russia, autumn 1941

7
Ju 88A-4 trop L1+HK of 2./LG 1, Derna, Libya, December 1941

8
Ju 88A-4 F1+AS of 8./KG 76, Orscha-Süd, Russia, December 1941

9
Ju 88C R4+C? of I./NJG 2, Gilze-Rijen, the Netherlands, late 1941/early 1942

Ju 88C-4 Wk-Nr 360219 R4+GM flown by Oberfeldwebel Wilhelm Beier, 4./NJG 2, Gilze-Rijen, the Netherlands, summer 1942

11
Ju 88A-4 R4+DK of I./NJG 2, Catania, Sicily, 1942

12
Ju 88C-6 R4+HH of 1./NJG 2, Catania, Sicily, 1942

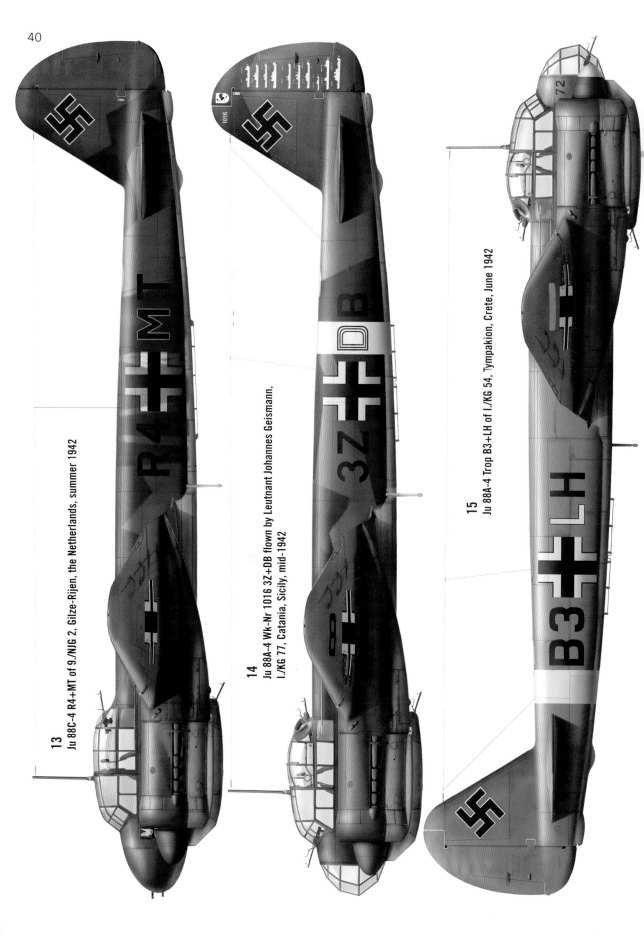

13
Ju 88C-4 R4+MT of 9./NJG 2, Gilze-Rijen, the Netherlands, summer 1942

14
Ju 88A-4 Wk-Nr 1016 3Z+DB flown by Leutnant Johannes Geismann,
I./KG 77, Catania, Sicily, mid-1942

15
Ju 88A-4 Trop B3+LH of I./KG 54, Tympakion, Crete, June 1942

16
Ju 88A-4 M2+AK of 2./KGr.106, Dinard, France, 1942

17
Ju 88C-4 R4+FM flown by Leutnant Wilhelm Beier, 10./NJG 1, Leeuwarden, the Netherlands, October 1942

18
Ju 88A-4 V4+FH of I./KG 1, Charkow-Woitschenko, Russia, winter 1942/43

19
Ju 88C-6 F1+KT flown by Oberleutnant Dieter Lukesch,
9./KG 76, Catania, Sicily, May 1943

20
Ju 88D-1 F6+DN, of 5.(F)./*Aufklärungsgruppe* 122,
Gosstkino, Russia, early 1943

21
Ju 88A-4 5K+FN of II./KG 3, Poltava, Russia, summer 1943

22
Ju 88C-6 F8+RY of 14./KG 40, Lorient, France, autumn 1943

23
Ju 88C-6 Wk-Nr 3060381 F8+BX of 13./KG 40, Lorient, France, September 1943

24
Ju 88A-4 3Z+AH of 1./KG 77, Orange-Caritat, France, spring/summer 1944

25
Ju 88A-4 3Z+EH of I./KG 77, Orange-Caritat, France, spring/summer 1944

26
Ju 88A-4 3Z+KS of 8./KG 77, Orange-Caritat, France, spring/summer 1944

27
Ju 88A-4 L1+BM of 4./LG 1, Glize-Rijen, the Netherlands, June 1944

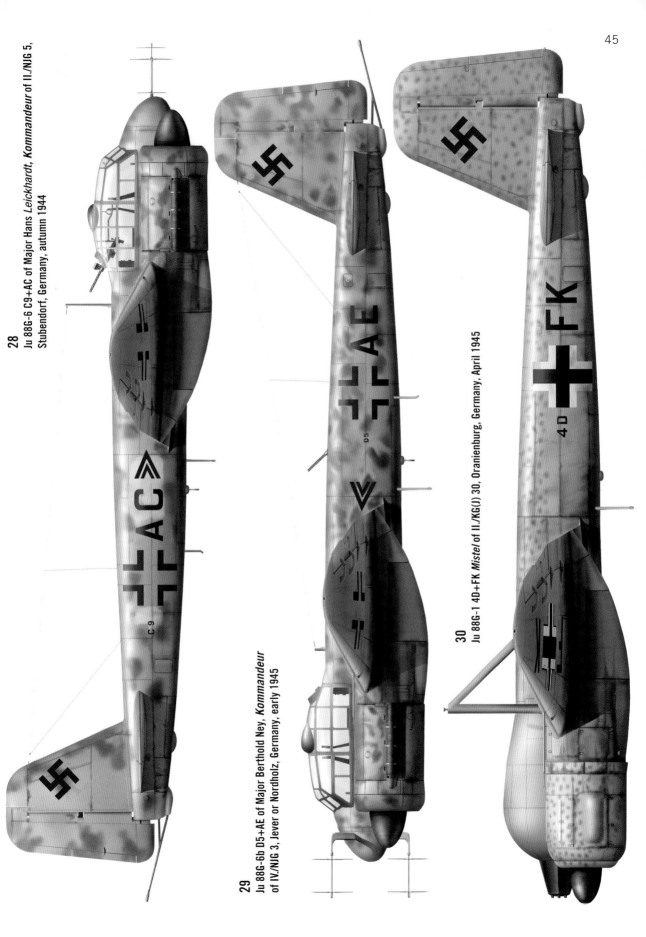

towards the airfield at nearby Upwood, before returning shortly thereafter to Oakington. He duly dropped ten bombs, damaging a Wellington in the process.

A recipient of the *Ehrenpokal*, Köster would move with I./NJG 2 to the Mediterranean towards the end of the year, where his score would continue to mount.

By the end of August 1941, I./NJG 2's crews had lodged claims for 135 aerial victories, the highest figure for a nightfighter unit at that time. However, these still relatively meagre successes failed to impress Hitler, who was only interested in the fact that RAF bomber incursions deeper into Reich airspace continued to take place. Furthermore, within the higher levels of the Luftwaffe command in the West, there was annoyance at Kammhuber, who was perceived as draining resources into his *Nachtjagddivision*, the functions of which were viewed as speculative. Kammhuber's plans for expansion of the *Fernnachtjäger* were foiled, being halted at one *Gruppe*.

Furthermore, shortly after the news that Hans Hahn had been lost on 11/12 October 1941, Kammhuber informed the shocked crews of I./NJG 2 that they were being transferred to Sicily. It seemed to the men of the *Fernnachtjäger* that their efforts over England had been marginalised, seemingly counting for very little.

Instead, the Luftwaffe wanted the Ju 88Cs sent to the Mediterranean, where they would be deployed as air escort for convoys carrying supplies to the *Deutsches Afrikakorps*. Thus, the Junkers arrived at their new base of Catania, on Sicily, in mid-November, retaining their *Englandblitz* emblems and all-black intruder colour schemes, on to which were overpainted yellow identification panels on their engine undersides and white theatre fuselage bands. For the second half of November the six Ju 88C-2s and C-4s of 2./NJG 2 under Hauptmann Heinz Harmstorff were detached and sent to Benghazi, in Libya, where they functioned under the tactical control of the *Fliegerführer Afrika*. However, by the 28th, the *Staffel* had returned to Catania. Harmstorff had a lucky escape when he was forced to land his C-4 under emergency conditions after his

Photographed here in late 1942 after the award of the Knight's Cross, Alfons Köster was credited with 11 night intruder victories over England while flying with I./NJG 2, followed by five more in the Mediterranean. He was another ace who would survive until 1945, but not survive the war. Köster was killed on 7 January 1945 while with IV./NJG 3 when his Ju 88G collided with the roof of a farmhouse in fog close to Varel-Obenstrohe airfield

Appearing oddly incongruous under the broiling Sicilian sun, this Ju 88C-6 nightfighter of I./NJG 2 is finished in a standard all-black nocturnal camouflage and carries the *Englandblitz* emblem on its nose. The only concession to its new theatre of operations is a white half-band applied to the rear fuselage

Luftwaffe officers in tropical uniform walk away from an all-black Ju 88C nightfighter of I./NJG 2 somewhere in the Mediterranean, the man on the left holding a camera. The *Gruppe's* aircraft shifted bases regularly as, in addition to operating as fighters, they provided convoy escort and reconnoitred for submarines

Leutnant Heinz Rökker (seen here as a Hauptmann after the award of the Oak Leaves to the Knight's Cross on 12 March 1945 for his 60th victory) was one of the first Mediterranean nightfighter aces of I./NJG 2. Flying with 1. *Staffel*, he claimed six enemy bombers (five Wellingtons, one of which was not confirmed, and a Beaufort) shot down between 20 June 1942 and 19 April 1943. They were the first victories in an eventual tally of 61

aircraft had been badly hit by anti-aircraft fire on 23 November.

Just before the move to Sicily, command of I./NJG 2 had changed when Hülshoff was appointed *Kommodore* of the *Geschwader* and Major Erich Jung became *Gruppenkommandeur*.

The Ju 88 crews found their new operating environment challenging, and they were stretched in their tasks, which invariably led to losses. In addition to convoy escort, I./NJG 2 conducted intruder missions over Malta as well as flying 'routine' nightfighter patrols over North Africa, Sicily and Crete. It was draining work, and aside from long-range intruder missions, the flying often involved circling at night for hours over Axis convoys, or escorting Luftwaffe transport aircraft, or flying daylight missions and even, on occasions, hunting for enemy submarines.

The *Gruppe's* victory success rate declined as losses grew, while there were few, if any, deliveries of fresh Ju 88Cs. In February 1942 I./NJG 2 reported just ten aircraft on strength, of which six were usually serviceable at any one time. As a measure of assistance, Bf 110s of III./ZG 26 would join I./NJG 2 in circling the convoys.

From April 1942 elements of I./NJG 2 were scattered all over the Mediterranean, with detachments at Benina, Berca, Derna, Benghazi, El Quasaba and Kastelli on Crete, although the unit's main base remained at Catania. By then the unit was also operating a small number of new C-6s, which differed very little from the older C-2s aside from improved performance from their Jumo 211J engines.

Leutnant Heinz Rökker from Oldenburg, in Niedersachsen, had joined the 1./NJG 2 in May 1942. He had enlisted in the Luftwaffe in October 1939, and in September 1941 Rökker was posted to *Nachtjagdschule* 1 for operational training. He flew operationally for the first time on 20 June 1942, and in the process shot down a Beaufort of No 217 Sqn that he had spotted flying low over the sea near Crete. He only avoided colliding with the bomber by throttling back hard, before going after another Beaufort. This aircraft put up stiff opposition, however, with Sgt J Hutcheson and his crew inflicting 25 hits on Rökker's Ju 88C. The German pilot eventually broke off the fight after 35 minutes.

Having claimed Wellingtons destroyed on 25 and 26 June, Rökker encountered yet another Vickers bomber at a height of 600 m just before midnight on the 28th near the Egyptian port of Mersa Matruh while flying from Derna, in Libya. Compensating again for the speed of the Wellington, he slowly closed on his target. Rökker's fighter was eventually spotted and the cockpit area of the Ju 88C-6 hit by defensive fire that inflicted splinter wounds on the crew. After climbing away to base, having reportedly watched the Wellington make a belly-landing (no losses were recorded by the RAF that night, however), Rökker suddenly noticed that the water and oil temperatures of his Junkers' right engine had risen dramatically. At the same time, the left engine burst into flames while the aircraft was only 200 m above the ground. As Rökker related;

'The pilot of a Ju 88 had only a remote chance of survival if he tried to bail out through the ventral gondola at so low an altitude, and if he tried to get out through the cabin roof he was in great danger of hitting the tail fin, so I decided to make a belly-landing in the desert. To make matters worse, as happened almost every night, a sheet of fog had formed on the ground. We had to rely on fliers' luck to find a suitable spot on the desert floor. The landing flaps were lowered successfully, and in that way we came down towards the ground in a state of tense awareness.'

Rökker had force-landed 60 km west of Mersa Matruh. The crew left the aircraft via the rear exit, by which stage the left engine was no longer burning. Although they closely examined the damaged aircraft, Rökker and his men could only locate bullet holes in each engine and one in the cabin area. The airmen were soon discovered by German soldiers, but as Rökker recalled, 'It was with heavy hearts that we took leave of our fine Ju 88. It felt to me as if I was having to leave a badly wounded comrade behind'.

Meanwhile, back at Gilze-Rijen, intruder work was continued to a less frequent extent over England by II./NJG 2. The *Gruppe* had been formed in November 1941 and equipped with the Ju 88 from the outset. On 30 June 1942, Oberfeldwebel Rolf Bussmann decided to load up his Junkers with bombs and then fly out over the North Sea, where he infiltrated a returning RAF bomber stream. He claimed to have shot down a No 405 'Canadian' Sqn Halifax, before proceeding to cross the English coast and unload his bombs on their airfield at Pocklington in Yorkshire.

In November, the Ju 88Cs of II./NJG 2 under Hauptmann Herbert Bönsch arrived at Comiso from Gilze-Rijen to operate over the Mediterranean under the tactical control of II. *Fliegerkorps*.

Serving beside Heinz Rökker in the Mediterranean – and for most of the war – was his radio operator, Carlos Nugent. Joining I./NJG 2 in May 1942, he is credited with 147 combat missions and participation in 61, possibly 62, night victories with Rökker. On 17 April 1945, Nugent became one of the few radio operators to receive the Knight's Cross

The Ju 88C-6 of Leutnant Heinz Rökker of 1./NJG 2 at an unidentified base in the Mediterranean. The aircraft has been finished in an overwater scribble camouflage and has no flame-dampers fitted, suggesting its deployment in daylight operations, although *Lichtenstein* radar aerials are fitted

CHAPTER THREE

CONQUEST OF THE EAST

A Ju 88A-5 of I./KG 3 is guided to a stop by a member of the ground personnel at an airfield in Russia in 1941. The *Gruppe* operated under II. *Fliegerkorps*, carrying out missions in the central sector of the front, including raids on Moscow. The *Gruppe*'s emblem of a red lightning flash over a white shield has been applied to the nose, and the spinner tips bear the same colours

In the spring of 1941, as the prospect of a vast military undertaking in the East grew ever closer, Adolf Hitler and the German High Command were drawn to deal with what they perceived as an uncertain situation in the Balkans. To see through its military endeavours and to fuel an ever-expanding Reich, Germany needed Rumanian oil. At that point in time, the Rumanian oil fields were relatively secure – they were beyond the range of the nearest British aircraft based in Palestine and Egypt. However, if Britain decided to escalate its military presence in Greece, then Italy would be forced to fight for its occupation of that country, and to the Germans, judging by Italy's recent record in North Africa, that could be questionable. The whole Balkan Peninsula need securing.

The Germans were helped in their cause by the fact that the countries bordering Greece to the north, Bulgaria and Albania, were already members of the Axis, and on 25 March, the Yugoslavian Regent, Prince Paul, had signed the Tripartite Pact, thus placing his country under German influence. On 13 December 1940, Hitler issued a directive for what was coded Operation *Marita* in which he foresaw a German occupation of Greece in order to prevent the 'establishment of an air base which would threaten Italy in the first place, and, incidentally, the Rumanian oil fields'. These, in the context of Hitler's longer-term grand strategy, were high stakes.

The ground plan for *Marita* hinged around offensive operations in Greece and Yugoslavia conducted by the German 2. and 12. *Armee*. These armies were to be supported by the air units of *Luftflotte* 4 under the command of the Austrian *General der Flieger* Alexander Löhr, headquartered in Vienna.

By mid-March, most air units, amounting to some 400 aircraft, slated for operations directed at Greece had been moved into Rumania and Bulgaria. However, what the Germans did not anticipate was that the Yugoslavians would rise up in revolution in Belgrade against their government, which had been cordial towards Nazi Germany. This sudden danger to the German right flank forced a decision to attack Belgrade and, despite the consequences and ensuing world reaction to the bombing of the city, German military planners wanted a swift campaign in the Balkans so that forces could be returned quickly in readiness for operations further east. The crushing of any resistance in Belgrade would ensure that this would be the case and therefore the bombing, as a military operation, was viewed as entirely justified.

On the eve of the attack, Löhr's Order of Battle numbered 12 *Gruppen* of bombers, with some directly subordinate to the *Luftflotte*, while others were assigned to two *Fliegerkorps*. Seven of these *Gruppen*, plus associated Staff flights, were equipped with the Ju 88. The *Stab*, I., II. and III./KG 51 under Major Hans Bruno Schulze-Heyn were based at Wiener-Neustadt in eastern Austria, while a single *Gruppe*, I./LG 1, under Hauptmann Kuno Hoffmann, at Plovdiv-Krumovo in Bulgaria, fell under *General der Flieger* Wolfram *Freiherr* von Richthofen's VIII. *Fliegerkorps*. Away to the west, in Sicily, as part of Generalleutnant Hans Geisler's X. *Fliegerkorps*, were the *Stab*, II. and III./LG 1 under the overall command of Oberst Friedrich-Karl Knust at Catania, as well as III./KG 30, which had moved to Gerbini in February, and is believed to have been led at the time by Major Martin Schumann.

Some of these units, such as KG 51, had begun to take delivery of the new Ju 88A-4, which was to serve as a mainstay until the war's end. Powered for the most part by 12-cylinder, liquid-cooled inline Jumo 211J-1 engines that produced 1401 hp on take-off, the A-4 would provide the Luftwaffe with a first-class, high-speed bomber that was stable and multi-functional, and one of the finest aircraft designs to emerge from wartime German drawing boards. The increased performance provided by the Jumo 211J-1 meant that the Ju 88's armour, bomb load and fuel tankage was increased correspondingly. The bomber was now capable of a maximum speed of 475 km/h, representing a gain of around 25 km/h over the A-5, with a range of 2500 km/h.

The Ju 88A-4 was able to carry a short-range bomb load of 3600 kg, although the ordnance could be interchanged with the fuel load, internally and externally. There was also a change to the design of the rear cockpit's defensive armament (B-*Stand*) with a pair of 7.92 mm MG 81 belt-fed machine guns mounted in circular panels, which themselves formed part of a revised, bulged rear canopy. Additional armament comprised a single MG 81 in the A-*Stand*, with an MG 81Z (*Zwilling* – twin) gun arrangement in the rear gondola *Bola* C-*Stand* and ammunition boxes for these weapons stored around the cabin, which accommodated the crew of four. Further weapons configurations could be introduced for mission-specific purposes or to suit crew preference at unit level. Navigational and radio equipment was also updated.

Arguably, it would be the Luftwaffe's eastern campaigns that would define the Ju 88A-4 as a combat aircraft. In the interim, however, the crews of KG 51 became acquainted with the new variant by making training flights from Wiener-Neustadt over the Danube and deep into Hungary and Rumania. By 5 April, KG 51 fielded a total of 88 Ju 88s, of which 60 per cent were usually serviceable. The following day, aircraft from the *'Edelweiss' Geschwader*, loaded with high-explosive (HE) and incendiary bombs, took part in the assault on Belgrade under the code name Operation *Strafgericht* (Retribution), in which the Yugoslav capital was subjected to bombing waves at 15-minute intervals, each lasting for approximately 20 minutes. The attacks caused significant destruction and thousands were killed, the city's population swollen by visitors from other towns and villages there to celebrate Palm Sunday. As far as Löhr was concerned, the raid was in direct support of the army.

Over the coming days, attacks on other towns were carried out. On 13 April, for example, III./KG 51 flew 29 sorties and dropped 28 800-kg bombs. In nine days of operations over Yugoslavia, III./KG 51, under the command of future Knight's Cross-holder Major Walter Marienfeld, flew 148 sorties, covering just over 145,000 km and dropped 154,000 kg of HE, incendiary and fragmentation bombs. The *Gruppe* suffered four operational losses, and one crew claimed the destruction of a Yugoslav air force Hurricane over Mostar on 12 April.

On 5 April, II. and III./LG 1 transferred from Catania to Grottaglie, from where, over the coming days, their Ju 88A-5s attacked targets in Yugoslavia. These included troop positions, staff headquarters, barracks and bridges in the Sarajevo, Skopje and Mostar areas, with each Junkers loaded with one S-500 and three SC-250 bombs. The next day, however, the two *Gruppen* returned to Catania, marking the end of their involvement in operations over the Balkans.

Meanwhile, Hoffmann's I./LG 1 had moved to Plovdiv-Krumovo, from where it was intended to launch attacks on the Rupel Pass, immediately south of the Greek-Bulgarian border. On 7 April, flying in very bad weather in *Staffel*-strength formations, the Ju 88s bombed rail lines, railway buildings and roads in the Veles area. The targets were difficult to locate because of the weather, and during the afternoon they shifted to the Skopje area. On the morning of the 8th, acting in support of *Panzergruppe* 1, the *Gruppe* mounted formation diving attacks against crossroads and the approach roads to several towns. One crew to enjoy particular success at this time against enemy transport columns, as well as in ground-strafing troop concentrations, was that of Feldwebel Otto Leupert. Eventually decorated with the Knight's Cross on 22 January 1943 for anti-shipping work off North Africa and around Malta, Leupert had honed his skills in the Balkans.

At 1230 hrs on 14 April, around 30 Ju 88s of I./LG 1 took off from Krumovo in close formation to dive-bomb ships in Piraeus, each aircraft loaded with three SC-500s. The harbour was defended by strong anti-aircraft batteries, and RAF Hurricanes also patrolled the skies. Despite these threats, the crews entered their dives and Leupert managed to sink a 10,000-GRT freighter. A 6000-GRT vessel bombed by Feldwebel Georg Sattler was thrown against the quayside. Next morning, shortly after dawn,

25 aircraft from I./LG 1 mounted another raid on Piraeus, and this time each Junkers carried one SC-1000 and one SC-500. Despite running into Hurricanes of No 80 Sqn and Blenheims of No 4 Sqn, the Ju 88s broke through the air screen and anti-aircraft fire to reach the harbour. On this occasion, Feldwebel Leupert struck at port installations, although when the Junkers turned for home, six Greek and British vessels had also been sunk for the loss of two Ju 88s.

A Ju 88A-4, believed to be from 6./KG 76, passes overhead during Operation *Barbarossa* in 1941. The *Staffel* was one of those supporting the advance of Army Group North through Lithuania and Latvia towards Leningrad. The aircraft carries a yellow theatre identification fuselage band and is equipped with an MG/FF cannon in the forward gondola

Leupert was unlucky on the 16th when, during an attack on Volos harbour, he failed to hit another freighter after having dropped an SC-1000 and SC-500 from a height of 1000 m.

Missions continued in much the same manner through to the end of the campaign in the Balkans, by which time LG 1 had been responsible for the sinking of, or damage to, vessels totalling at least 43,000 GRT. However, the *Geschwader* had lost nine aircraft and several crews. These successes and losses would be quickly overshadowed in the coming weeks by the prospect of war looming further to the east.

By the summer of 1941, the whole of Continental Europe, bar Soviet Russia, was Axis, Axis-occupied or neutral. Germany's victories prior to Operation *Barbarossa* swept away the prospect of any significant military opposition to Hitler, even from Britain, while the USA remained distant in its isolation and neutrality. Thus, with his political and military position secure, Adolf Hitler was free to embark upon the greatest invasion in history.

The foundation of Operation *Barbarossa* rested on three mighty Army Groups that would strike deep into the Soviet Union, their size and power dwarfing any previous German operations. To the north, *Heeresgruppe Nord* (Army Group North) would attack from northern Poland through Lithuania and Latvia, link up with the Finnish Army, push into the Soviet North and Northwest Fronts and aim for Leningrad. To the right of Army Group North was *Heeresgruppe Mitte* (Centre), which would thrust east from the Bug River, aiming for Minsk, encircling and destroying Soviet forces in Belorussia and continuing to Smolensk. To the south, spanning a vast starting position stretching from southern Poland, across the Carpathians to the Danube, was *Heeresgruppe Süd* (South). This army group was to advance through the Ukraine towards Kiev and the Dnieper, pressing on to Kharkov, the Donets and the Don against the Soviet Southwest and South Fronts, with the Caucasus as its ultimate objective. The German start line stretched for around 1600 km and was aimed against a Russian front running from Leningrad to Odessa for 2400 km.

With 153 divisions containing almost 3.6 million German and Axis troops, 3600 tanks and assault guns, 600,000 motor vehicles, 625,000 horses and 7100 artillery pieces, these three Army Groups formed the most powerful military strike force in European history.

Reichsmarschall Hermann Göring personally awarded Dresden-born Stabsfeldwebel Rudolf Nacke of 7./KG 76 with the Knight's Cross on 23 July 1941, shortly after the commencement of Operation *Barbarossa*. Nacke became extremely proficient at attacking small, pinpoint targets in England in 1940 and later saw action on the northern and southern sectors of the Russian Front before KG 76 was moved south to support the advance on Stalingrad. His crew also shot down two Soviet fighters prior to the *Gruppe* being transferred to the Mediterranean in November 1942

Supporting the Army Groups, the Luftwaffe fielded three *Luftflotten*. Covering Army Group North was *Luftflotte* 1 under Generaloberst Alfred Keller. The *Flotte*, which had a strength of 592 combat and transport aircraft, of which 453 were operational, numbered just one complete *Korps* in the form of Generalleutnant Helmuth Förster's I. *Fliegerkorps*, which, aside from the small *Stab*/KG 1, was equipped entirely with Ju 88s drawn from II. and III./KG 1 (56 serviceable Ju 88s), *Stab*, I., II. and III./KG 76 (66), *Stab*, I., II. and III./KG 77 (67) and, under the *Fliegerführer Ostsee*, KGr.806 (18). These units would partake in operations to support the Army Group as it advanced from East Prussia towards the Dvina River and on to Leningrad. They were to assist *Panzergruppe* 4 in its advance along a front of 200 km and a depth (to Leningrad) of some 850 km, with much of their ordnance formed of anti-personnel fragmentation bombs.

Providing air support to Army Group Centre was *Luftflotte* 2, the strongest of the air fleets, commanded by Generalfeldmarschall Kesselring. It had a strength of 1367 combat and transport aircraft, of which 994 were operational, and was to move east in the direction of Moscow with the Army Group. Alongside the Do 17s and He 111s of KG 2 and KG 53, the Ju 88 contingent comprised the *Stab*, I. and II./KG 3 (66 serviceable machines). Most of *Luftflotte* 2's *Kampfgruppen* would also be given anti-personnel fragmentation bombs for army support.

To the south, Generaloberst Löhr's *Luftflotte* 4 was assigned to Army Group South and included *General der Flieger* Robert *Ritter* von Greim's V. *Fliegerkorps* in the Lublin-Zamosc area, which numbered *Stab*, I., II. and III./KG 51 (81 serviceable Ju 88s) and *Stab*, I. and II./KG 54 (65). These bombers were to back up *Panzergruppe* 1's advance towards the Dnieper so as to prevent Russian forces from escaping across the river. In addition, attacks would be made to paralyse and neutralise the Soviet Air Force and to knock out communications centres and command headquarters.

The sheer scale of *Barbarossa*, the lightning speed of the initial German advance, the confidence of the German forces and the colossal numbers of aircraft and vehicles involved on both sides meant that very quickly reputations were made within the ranks of the Luftwaffe bomber crews. Furthermore, the Ju 88 was something of a 'new shock' to the Russians, for they were already familiar with other German aircraft types having encountered them during the Spanish Civil War. Yet it was the experience of some Ju 88 crews that if and when they did encounter the enemy in the air, Soviet fighter pilots often initially elected not to engage the Junkers.

Operating a mix of Ju 88A-4s and A-5s, II./KG 1, under the command of Hauptmann Otto Stams, prosecuted a campaign of harassment against the Russian supply routes, with the road and railway transport network being hit hard as the *Wehrmacht* advanced north to Leningrad. Also, throughout June and July, Soviet airfields were attacked in the Riga and Pskov areas, cargo ships bombed in the Baltic and Gulf of Finland and on 3 July, the *Gruppe* bombed Liepāja (Libau) and Leningrad itself. In the first month of the campaign in Russia, II./KG 1 destroyed more than 200 enemy aircraft on the ground

Leading by example, Stams, who had first started flying powered aircraft in 1926, carried out many missions against bridges and transport targets. Hailing from the province of Posen, Otto Stams trained at the *Deutsche Verkehrsfliegerschule* (German Commercial Pilot School) from January 1927 and became a military pilot when he joined I./KG 152 'Hindenburg' in November 1937. Because of his experience, he became that unit's Technical Officer and later flew missions in Poland.

Joining the newly formed KG 1, into which elements of KG 152 had been integrated, Stams was appointed *Staffelkapitän* of 7. *Staffel*. He led this unit in attacks against airfield and factories in Great Britain in 1940, flying the He 111.

It was in Russia that he excelled, however, leading II./KG 1 as its *Kommandeur*. While on a sortie on 27 June 1941, striking at rail targets, he destroyed two trains. However, Stams' Ju 88A-5 was hit by ground fire, as a result of which he was badly wounded in his left leg. Nevertheless, he managed to fly his bomber and its crew safely back to base at Saborovka.

Stams was awarded the Knight's Cross on 1 August 1941 in recognition of his leadership and successes in the East, but he was no longer able to fly on operations due to the wounds he had received on 27 June. He was subsequently appointed *Kommandeur* of the *Eprobungsstelle der Luftwaffe* at Karlshagen, then Peenemünde and, later, in October 1943, the test centre for air-dropped weapons at Jesau. Stams ended the war as the *Kommodore* of an aircraft ferrying unit, having flown some 50 combat missions.

Adolf Kraus from Rödelmaier, near Neustadt an der Saale, was 25 years old when he joined Stams' *Gruppe* in 4. *Staffel* in May 1941. Like so many German boys in the early 1930s, he had been a keen glider pilot and had joined the Luftwaffe in late 1936. After training, Kraus joined the *Erg.Staffel*/KG 1 before being assigned to 4./KG 1. As a member of Stams' *Gruppe*, Unteroffizier Kraus undertook missions directed at the Soviet supply routes in the northern sector of the front, as well as enemy strongpoints and supply dumps. He also sank three freighters on Lake Ladoga. By August 1942 he had been promoted to Oberfeldwebel and had flown no fewer than 350 combat missions in 15 months.

Kraus and his crew survived being shot down twice between August 1941 and May 1942, although they were all wounded on the second occasion. On 30 September 1942, however, after taking off from Siwerskaja, the left engine of his Ju 88A-4 caught fire and although Kraus attempted to land, the aircraft stalled and crashed into a forest near the airfield, killing all on board. Adolf Kraus was posthumously awarded the Knight's Cross on 25 October of that year in recognition of his outstanding service record.

Three weeks prior to Kraus' death, KG 1 had suffered another serious blow when, on 3 September 1942, *Geschwaderkommodore* Major Hans

In the far north of the Eastern Front, KG 30 used its Ju 88s to prosecute a campaign against the convoys to Murmansk, as well as against the port itself and its railway connections. Flying from Banak, Hauptmann Konrad Kahl, a veteran of the campaign against England, undertook several such missions, including attacks against the infamous convoy PQ-17. Kahl is seen here in the foreground during the official award ceremony of the Knight's Cross at Banak on 18 August 1942. Decorated in recognition of his anti-convoy work, he flew a total of 220 combat missions (*John Weal*)

Oberfeldwebel Friedrich Kralemann (seated in the centre, behind the flowers) of 5./KG 3 is treated to a cake and Sekt along with a serenade following his completion of 200 combat missions, possibly at Schatalowka or Orscha-Süd on the central sector of the Russian Front, in the early summer of 1942. Kralemann's log of enemy transport destroyed during the opening months of *Barbarossa* was extraordinary – 16 tanks, 111 trucks, seven locomotives and 26 trains. He also destroyed 58 Soviet aircraft on the ground as well as numerous enemy gun positions. On 30 June 1941, Kralemann's Ju 88A-4 was hit by ground fire in the Moscow area and he force-landed in enemy territory. He and his crew managed to return on foot to German lines, but on 10 September 1942, Kralemann suffered the loss of his left eye as a result of shell splinters. The severity of his injuries saw him removed from operational flying, and Kralemann was eventually awarded the Knight's Cross on 29 October 1943. He succumbed to his wounds four weeks later. Note the armourer working in the background close to the open door at the rear of the *Bola* (*John Weal*)

Keppler had collided with a Bf 109 while on a reconnaissance flight near Lake Ladoga. He and his crew, as well as the fighter pilot, were killed in the accident. A very experienced aviator, Keppler, like Otto Stams, was a product of the *Deutsche Verkehrsfliegerschule*, and from May 1939 he had served as *Staffelkapitän* of 2./KG 51. Flying combat missions during the campaign in the West in 1940, he was appointed to command 7./KG 1 following spells firstly as a liaison officer between the Luftwaffe and the *Kriegsmarine* and then as adjutant to *General der Flieger* Jeschonnek. Once on the Eastern Front Keppler and his crew accounted for the destruction of four trains, four artillery positions and 14 tanks. Keppler had flown more than 300 missions prior to his death, having been awarded the Knight's Cross exactly two weeks before the accident.

Keppler's successor at the helm of KG 1 was Major Heinrich Lau. Born in 1911, Lau too had been trained at a commercial pilot's school and went on to fly courier missions with the *Legion Condor*. After subsequently serving with I./KG 254 and as a liaison officer to II. *Flakkorps*, Lau joined II./KG 30 in December 1939, with whom he began to fly the Ju 88 against British shipping in the North Sea. On 15 May 1940 he was appointed *Kapitän* of 1./KG 30, before taking command of the *Staffel's* parent *Gruppe* the following September. Lau was to suffer serious injuries in a motoring accident shortly after commencing his duties as *Kommandeur*, forcing him to spend several months in hospital recuperating. He returned to operations, but was then shot down in his Ju 88A-4 by an RAF nightfighter over Eindhoven airfield on 15 March 1941. Two of his crew were killed during this action.

When I./KG 30 was transferred to the far north in the summer of 1941, Lau soon chalked up an impressive combat record that saw him credited with the sinking of a Russian destroyer and the destruction of several trains near Murmansk. He later flew bombing missions around Stalingrad and over the Caucasus, but from March 1943 he retired from combat flying to take on successive staff positions with the *Angriffsführer England*, the *General der Kampfflieger*, the 3. *Jagddivision* and the *Kommando der Erprobungsstellen*. Heinrich Lau was awarded the Knight's Cross on 10 May 1943, having flown more than 200 combat missions. Having survived the war, he was killed in a flying accident in New Mexico in September 1956.

Following the first weeks of operations in Russia, Knight's Crosses would go to three other Ju 88 pilots – Ernst-Wilhelm Ihrig, Hans-Wilhelm Bender and Matthias Schwegler.

In the central sector of the front, I. and II./KG 3 conducted tactical operations with II. *Fliegerkorps* in support of the land advance, suppressing Soviet air power on the ground and therefore contributing to German air superiority. One pilot of 3./KG 3 who carved a fearsome reputation for low-level bombing and ground-attack work was Darmstadt-born Oberleutnant Ernst-Wilhelm Ihrig. Having joined the Luftwaffe during the mid-1930s, he was trained almost immediately as a bomber pilot and posted to KG 153, which was redesignated KG 3 in May 1939. Ihrig flew missions over Poland and France in the Do 17, with which the *Geschwader* was initially equipped, as well in the

Luftwaffe technicians remove important items and parts from Ju 88A-4 F1+AS of 8./KG 76 after it force-landed in snow-covered terrain in Russia during the winter of 1941/42. The aircraft has been covered in a temporary seasonal covering of white, although the *Staffel* emblem of a wasp over a red disc remains very visible. Although the aircraft was probably recovered, items such as radio equipment and guns were always needed, and emphasis placed on their quick salvage wherever possible

campaign against England. During the latter he was often chosen to fly lone, low-level night sorties against factories and specially selected targets.

Then, on the first day of Operation *Barbarossa*, while supporting the advance of the right wing of Army Group Centre in the Soviet-German border district of Poland, the then Leutnant Ihrig achieved something quite remarkable. Again flying a lone Ju 88A-5, he attacked the airfield at Pinsk in the southwest of the Soviet-occupied territory. During the course of six low-level runs across the field, he claimed the destruction of no fewer than 60 enemy aircraft on the ground, the Soviet 39th *Bistraya Bombardirovochniy Aviapolk* (Fast Bomber Air Regiment) of the 10th *Smeshannaya Aviatsionniy Diviziya* (Combined Aviation Division) alone losing 43 SB twin-engined bombers and five Pe-2s.

However, shortly after his attack, Ihrig's Ju 88, which was also carrying the *Staffelkapitän*, Major Günter Heinze as observer, was hit by anti-aircraft fire and he was forced down in enemy territory. Despite his gunner being fatally wounded, Ihrig, Heinze and the radio operator set off on foot, and after several days managed to return to German lines.

Ihrig soon succeeded Heinze as *Staffelkapitän* and embarked on regular and successful missions, leading his *Staffel* in attacks against Soviet transport, troop and vehicle targets. He received the Knight's Cross on 14 August 1941 in recognition of his operational successes and tactical leadership. On 7 December that year he was appointed to take over from Major Wladimir Graowass as *Kommandeur* of III./KG 3 during its conversion from the Do 17 to the Ju 88. Returning to the central front, Ihrig was lost on 30 November 1942 when his Ju 88A-14 was almost certainly hit by ground fire during a mission to the Beloy area. It is thought that he had flown around 300 missions by the time of his demise.

Aside from conducting tactical operations with II. *Fliegerkorps* in support of the ground advance, I. and II./KG 3 had been tasked with undertaking longer-range 'strategic' bombing missions against Moscow. The first raid took place on 21/22 July 1941, with others following over the coming months.

A week later, II. *Gruppe* almost lost one of its most accomplished pilots when the Ju 88A-5 flown by Oberfeldwebel Hans-Wilhelm Bender of 5. *Staffel* took a direct hit from anti-aircraft fire north of Roslavl. Bender's

His Knight's Cross visible, Oberleutnant Mathias Schwegler of 1./KG 51 smiles down at a small audience of military personnel and civilians from the cockpit of his Ju 88A-1 shortly after receiving the award in December 1941. He was the first recipient of the decoration in recognition of his successful operations over Dunkirk, England, the Balkans and the Soviet Union. Schwegler was shot down behind Russian lines in July 1941, although he and his crew made it back to German-held territory. He is credited with sinking 116,000 GRT of shipping in the English Channel and Black Sea (*John Weal*)

observer and radio operator were killed and shell splinters cut into the pilot's back and smashed his shoulder. Despite his wounds, Bender, who was flying his 125th mission, managed to coax the Junkers bomber back to the *Staffel*'s base at Orsha, where he made a wheels-up landing. The former policeman spent an extended period in hospital and never returned to operational flying. In recognition of his combat record, which included almost 100 missions flown over the West and England, Bender was awarded the Knight's Cross on 8 September 1941. He subsequently joined the Junkers *Flugzeugwerke* as an acceptance pilot.

In the south, by late 1941, for crews of KG 51, the long hot summer of advance towards the Crimea and the pouring autumn rains over Bessarabia had become distant memories as the weather turned into a bitter winter. One bright spot for the *Geschwader* was the celebration of its first Knight's Cross on 18 December when Oberleutnant Matthias 'Teddy' Schwegler of 1. *Staffel* was decorated in recognition of a string of successes, not least of which was the sinking of an enemy cruiser on the Black Sea.

Schwegler had joined III./KG 51 when war broke out, but did not fly his first operational sortie – a leaflet-dropping mission over France – until 6 November 1939. After his *Gruppe*'s conversion to the Ju 88 in May 1940, he partook successively in missions over Dunkirk, southern England and the Balkans. Appointed leader of 1./KG 51 in May 1941, Schwegler carried out attacks on British warships off Crete, and on one of these he damaged a destroyer. In Russia, he soon earned himself a reputation for leading many successful low-level bombing attacks against airfields, railway stations, junctions and bridges, as well as targeting enemy shipping on the Black Sea. After receiving the Knight's Cross, Schwegler was promoted to Hauptmann in February 1942 and spent the rest of the war as commander of various trials and training units. He was finally shot down and killed on 18 April 1945, by which point he had been credited with sinking 116,000 GRT of shipping in the English Channel and Black Sea.

Meanwhile, conditions for KG 51 at the turn of 1941/42 in southern Russia were becoming increasingly challenging. A member of III. *Gruppe* recorded;

'Winter set in. At last the times of grinding through the mud were over, and one could taxi again on the wide Russian runways without sinking in – even if it was bitterly cold. Continuing falls of snow and biting blizzards turned the country into a snow desert. Servicing had to be done all the time with numb hands. There was no suitable winter clothing.

The cold-starting procedure never seemed to go quite so well as the theory so confidently laid down in the Luftwaffe operating instructions. The mechanics had to start warming up at 2 am to make sure all aircraft would be ready for a dawn takeoff.'

On 15 January 1942, the *Sonderstab Krim* (Special Staff Crimea) was established as a tactical air command under *General der Flieger* Robert *Ritter* von Greim. It was tasked with rendering support to Generalfeldmarschall Erich von Manstein's 11. *Armee* as it attempted to force the Russians out of the Crimea.

The Ju 88s of KG 51 now operated under von Greim's direction, interdicting traffic on the road across the Kerch Straits and attacking Soviet supply shipping at both ends of the Crimea. For example, on 24 February aircraft from Major Ernst *Freiherr* von Bibra's III. *Gruppe* were tasked with bombing the battleship *Pariskaya Kommuna (Paris Commune)*, which had been blasting German positions. Such missions were difficult – amidst dense Soviet anti-aircraft fire, the Junkers crews failed to find the battleship, but they bombed a heavy cruiser instead just outside Yushnaja Bay. Up until the spring, elements of KG 51 flew regular missions against the bay, and to Balaclava, Kerch, Anapa, Novorossisk and other ports in the Caucasus.

On 14 March 1942, on the recommendation of Hauptmann Dietrich Peltz, the *Kommandeur* of the *Verbandsführerschule für Kampfflieger* (Bomber Unit Leaders' School) at Foggia, in Italy, III./KG 51 benefited from an extended visit by Hauptmann Werner Baumbach, by now one of the most famous names within the Luftwaffe. Peltz believed that Baumbach would be able to share some of his experience and expertise with the *'Edelweiss' Geschwader* in their over-water missions.

Since his first anti-shipping missions with II./KG 30 over Norway, Baumbach had been awarded the Knight's Cross on 8 May 1940 and travelled to Tokyo on behalf of the RLM. Returning home in early 1941, he had quickly gone back on to operations. In March of that year he was appointed *Staffelkapitän* of 4./KG 30 and his personal tally of shipping sunk while flying the Ju 88 amounted to 240,000 GRT at the end of February. On 14 July 1941, Baumbach was given the Oak Leaves to the Knight's Cross and was later assigned to a unit leader's course at the *Torpedoschule* in Foggia, before joining III./KG 51 on assignment.

He soon demonstrated his prowess by sinking a 10,000-GRT tanker in the port of Sevastopol on only his fourth mission over the Crimea. But even a bomber ace like Baumbach was daunted by the war over the Crimea, which he found to be 'something gruesome and horrific, fought with a fury which was quite exceptional even for this war', as he recorded in his memoirs;

'The Russians clung to their mother earth with unparalleled obstinacy. Our work at Sevastopol made the highest demands on men and material. Twelve, fourteen and even up to eighteen sorties were made daily by

Ground personnel hold a celebratory placard commemorating a *Staffel*'s 500th mission as the crew deplane from their Ju 88 at an unidentified unit in the East. The Junkers already bears a wreath emblem to mark the event. As the war in Russia ground on, such occasions became increasingly commonplace. Some sources state the aircraft shown here is a Ju 88D-1 of 1.(F)/33, in which case, the location would have been the central sector of the Eastern Front

RIGHT
This Ju 88A-14 flown by Hauptmann Klaus Häberlen (seen clasping a placard to mark his 300th battlefront flight), *Staffelkapitän* of 2./KG 51, has a 20 mm MG FF cannon installed in the ventral gondola. Note that the latter's bombsight window has been faired over in order to provide additional strengthening for the cannon fitment. The MG FF was used for both ground attack and anti-shipping work, this example also having a flash-suppressor fitted to its muzzle for night operations. The crew wear kapok life jackets, probably for missions over the Kuban bridgehead. Häberlen was decorated with the Knight's Cross on 20 June 1943 in recognition of his successful long-range combat missions (*John Weal*)

The Ju 88-equipped II./KG 76 achieved a landmark on 25 July 1942 when the *Gruppe* flew its 5000th mission in Russia – a mission flown by Oberleutnant Dr Friedrich Harries. He is seen here as a Hauptmann on the occasion of celebrating a personal landmark, namely the completion of 400 missions conducted against, or involving contact with, the enemy. Harries was awarded the Knight's Cross on 24 March 1943 while *Staffelführer* of 7./KG 76 when his mission tally stood at 300. He proved an adept pilot at bombing and strafing missions in the Crimea, the Caucasus, around Stalingrad and, from November 1942, in Tunisia

individual crews. A Ju 88 with fuel tanks full made three or four sorties without the crew stretching their legs. It meant tremendous wear and tear for the aircraft and the ground staff – those unknown soldiers who could not sleep a wink in those days and nights and were responsible for the safe condition of their machines.'

One successful anti-shipping pilot was Feldwebel Georg Fanderl of 1./KG 51. A Bavarian, 25 years of age at the time of operations in the Crimea, Fanderl was a veteran airman who had flown missions over England in 1940, then in the Balkans and Crete the following year. He was at least partly responsible for the sinking of a large merchantman off the Greek island, but was shot down during the process, being recovered from his dinghy by the British. Fanderl was fortunate enough to be freed by German *Fallschirmjäger* after the capture of Crete and returned to operations.

He became a ferocious low-level strike pilot in southern Russia, carrying out many attacks on troop convoys, vehicles, tanks, trains and railway targets, as well as badly damaging a Soviet cruiser and sinking a further 65,000 tons of shipping. He was awarded the Knight's Cross on 24 January 1942, but on 16 May that year he was shot down again when his Ju 88A-4 was attacked by Russian fighters south of Tomarovka. After recovering from wounds suffered in that engagement, Fanderl spent the final years of the war in the West serving with III./KG 6 and IV./KG 76. He is believed to have flown at least 180 missions.

On 18 June 1942, former instructor pilot Oberleutnant Ernst Hinrichs of 2./KG 51, who had once been forced down in enemy territory in September 1941, dived-bombed and sank an anti-aircraft barge in Severnaya Bay. He was awarded the Knight's Cross on 25 July for this feat. Shot down twice more over the Stalingrad sector, Hinrichs made it back to German lines on both occasions. His later career saw him in involved with operational training units and schools.

There was a blow for III./KG 51 when the *Gruppe's Kommandeur*, Major von Bibra, crashed in his Ju 88A-4 and was killed while on a mission near Slavyansk on 15 February 1943. The reasons behind why his aircraft came down remain unknown, but the loss of such an experienced unit leader under whose command the *Gruppe* had accounted for the destruction of thousands of enemy vehicles, tanks, guns and trains was a sobering example of what was increasingly becoming a sapping war of attrition.

Based at Zaparozhye for the first nine months of 1942, II./KG 51 operated under IV. *Fliegerkorps*. Railway-attack specialist Hauptmann Hellmuth Hauser of 5. *Staffel* was decorated with the Knight's Cross on 23 December 1942 after having personally claimed the destruction of 16 locomotives and 85 wagons, along with ten tanks, at least 100 vehicles and

20 artillery positions. Remarkably, Hauser and his crew also claimed six enemy aircraft destroyed in air combat and a further 20 on the ground. A veteran of earlier missions over England and the Balkans, Hauser later put his frontline experience to use in various tactical staff positions and eventually the OKL. He had flown 125 combat missions.

Elsewhere on the Eastern Front, 1942 brought glory to the other Ju 88 wings. Over the central sector in the early part of the year, Leutnant Benno Herrmann, the *Staffelkapitän* of 4./KG 76 who had flown several day and night missions over England in 1940, was credited with destroying 35 locomotives, and during a low-level attack on an enemy airfield, ten aircraft on the ground. On one occasion in February 1942, Herrmann's Junkers was rammed by a Soviet fighter, which his gunner then succeeded in shooting down. Herrmann duly managed to get the damaged Ju 88 back to base. The Knight's Cross came to the veteran bomber pilot on 10 June.

Hauptmann Peter-Paul Breu, the *Kommandeur* of II./KG 3 and an experienced 'train-killer' credited with the destruction of 34 troop trains, often chose to fly a cannon-armed Ju 88C-6 for his strafing work. On one occasion in July he had observed Soviet armour massing to attempt to break through German lines near Kirov. Breu quickly reported what he had seen and his *Gruppe* managed to stop the enemy incursion, destroying 26 tanks in the process. Breu received the Knight's Cross on 2 October 1942, having flown 250 missions in Russia.

Often, the amount of ground-attack destruction wreaked by Ju 88 crews was colossal. The commander of Breu's 6. *Staffel* was Leutnant Joachim Gey from Engelsdorf, near Leipzig. Between July-December 1942 while operating over the central section sector, Gey accounted for no fewer than 34 tanks, 82 trucks and 40 horse-drawn vehicles in the Rhzev area. He received the Knight's Cross on 21 June 1943.

Hauptmann Siegfried Barth, *Staffelkapitän* of 4./KG 51, poses for a photograph shortly after receiving his Knight's Cross on 2 October 1942. He flew countless missions against England and the Soviet Union. In Russia, Barth led his *Staffel* in regular, low-level attacks on transport and airfield targets in the southern sector. He is seen here wearing the Knight's Cross, the *Deutsches Kreuz in Gold*, the clasp with pendant for 400 missions, the Iron Cross First Class and ribbon for Second, the Wound Badge and the Pilot's Badge (*Author's collection*)

The *Staffelkapitän* of 7./KG 76, Hauptmann Dr Friedrich Harries (left), and Hauptmann Dieter Lukesch, *Kapitän* of 9. *Staffel*, were both Ju 88 stalwarts. Although this photograph was probably taken in the Mediterranean in early 1943, both men were Eastern Front veterans, Lukesch having sunk 12 tankers and two cargo vessels along the River Volga. He had been awarded the Knight's Cross in December 1941 for his operations in Russia and would go on to receive the Oak Leaves in October 1944. He would end the war flying the Ar 234 jet bomber

LEFT
Luftwaffe personnel gather in front of a Ju 88C-6 *Zerstörer* undergoing maintenance at an unknown location. The gun nose has been painted to appear from a distance as if it is glazed in a highly effective trompe l'oeil style – a unit-applied measure of deception that appeared on a number C-6s operating in the East against the Soviet transport network (*Author's collection*)

In III./KG 3 between May and September 1942, Feldwebel Karl Haupt, also from Leipzig, successfully shot up or bombed 22 trains, 12 railway stations, 55 trucks and an unknown number of fuel dumps. By 12 September Haupt had flown his 300th mission, and he was awarded the Knight's Cross on 3 February 1943, having flown 50 more.

The three *Gruppen* of KG 1 saw action at various times in the northern sector of the front. Several of the *Geschwader*'s officers became recipients of the Knight's Cross in August 1942, namely Oberleutnant Otto Edler von Ballasko of 10. *Staffel* on the 13th, Major Hans Keppler, commander of III. *Gruppe*, on the 20th, who was appointed *Geschwaderkommodore* the same day following the death of Oberstleutnant Peter Schemmell, and Oberleutnant Hans Sumpf, *Staffelkapitän* of 5./KG 1, posthumously also on the 20th. Collectively, these three pilots were responsible for the destruction of at least 27 locomotives, 140 wagons, 112 vehicles, 163 tanks, two bridges and six artillery positions in 1942.

These accomplishments were countered, however, by the loss of Major Herbert Lorch, the *Kommandeur* of II./KG 1, who was killed, along with his radio operator and gunner, when his Ju 88A-4 was shot down by Russian fighters southeast of Kolodesy on 19 August. Lorch was a veteran of the *Reichswehr* years and had flown over Poland and the West. He had undertaken more than 200 combat missions, many at low level, and accounted personally for five artillery batteries and many tanks, locomotives and vehicles. He was awarded the Knight's Cross after his death on 5 January 1943.

Before the onset of a terrible winter, meteorologically and militarily, KG 1 also saw the decoration being awarded to 25-year-old Feldwebel Kurt Mevissen of 9. *Staffel*, who gained a reputation for his daring attacks on enemy airfields and troop assembly points. While carrying out a dive-bombing attack on the ships of the Soviet Baltic Fleet at Kronstadt on 21 September 1941, he achieved a near miss on the battleship *Oktyabrskaya Revolutsiya* (*October Revolution*). He was awarded the Knight's Cross on 19 September, having flown more than 320 missions and in recognition of his tally of 11 tanks, 50 vehicles, nine trains and 50 horse-drawn wagons destroyed.

Just over two weeks later, the award was given to Oberleutnant Erich Taeger of 7. *Staffel*, another 'England veteran' who, in Russia, had chalked up around 100 vehicles, 11 trains and 16 tanks destroyed in around 300 missions. Taeger, a former technical officer of III./KG 1, was a tough airman who frequently took on lone, low-level special missions involving attacks on enemy headquarters, railway junctions or bridges. On one such mission, four days after the launch of *Barbarossa*, Taeger flew

700 km behind enemy lines to attack the Valogda-Arkhangelsk railway line.

By mid-November 1942 the southern sector of the German front stretched from Voronezh in the north to Elista and Essentuki in the south, curving back to Novorossisk on the Black Sea – a vast area of conquest taken in just six months. In the centre of this line was Stalingrad, most of which 6. *Armee* had taken in fierce fighting in October. However, on the morning of 19 November, as Hitler and his generals were distracted by the *Torch* landings in Tunisia, the Soviet Southwestern and Don

Hauptmann Ernst Fach of 9.(*Eis*)/KG 3 is hoisted on to the shoulders of groundcrew at Poltawa in April 1943 upon the successful completion of 300 missions conducted against, or involving contact with, the enemy. His Ju 88C-6 can be seen behind with the emblem of KG 3 on its nose. Also just visible to the right of the insignia is the wing of the flying railway wheel emblem of 9.(*Eis*)/KG 3 (*Author's collection*)

Fronts, followed the next day by the Stalingrad Front, launched Operation *Uranus*, a counter-offensive involving more than one million men that was designed to trap 6. *Armee* within the shell-shattered ruins of Stalingrad. By 23 November the encirclement of 6. *Armee* was complete when the Soviet Southwestern and Stalingrad Fronts met near Kalach, trapping 20 German and two Rumanian divisions totalling some 280,000 men and beginning one of the most wretched battles in military history, which would bleed 6. *Armee* dry amidst the most appalling conditions.

The Luftwaffe fought desperately to keep the skies over and around the beleaguered city free and the troops on the ground supplied, but it was an insurmountable task. As Ju 52/3ms assisted by He 111 bombers did their best to maintain supplies to 6. *Armee*, the Ju 88s of I. and III./KG 51 based at the large airfield of Tatsinskaya under the tactical control of VIII. *Fliegerkorps* did their best to maintain offensive sorties against Russian positions around the city. Conditions could not have been worse in this, the second gruelling Russian winter – the crews and their mechanics existed in dugouts, somehow hollowed out of the frozen ground. As the *Geschwader* historian has recorded;

'Cold, snow and a violent, icy wind made life in the dugouts difficult; the temperature often dropped to zero, and sometimes as low as -30°F. The technical side had a particularly hard time of it; they had to get up in the middle of the night to shovel the snow away from the aircraft and warm them up. Frostbite was especially common among the technicians, who had to check radios, bomb-release mechanisms and engines – tasks which could not be done in thick gloves. The guns froze up, oil froze solid and the situation was desperate.'

Despite this, men like Oberfeldwebel Albert Spieth of 3./KG 51 continued to fly bombing raids in atrocious weather. Impervious to the conditions, on numerous occasions, Spieth and his crew were able to seek out Soviet positions for attack despite the terrain being difficult to monitor. The sight of a bomb-laden Ju 88 flying low overhead towards enemy lines gave cheer to the desolate German troops in Stalingrad. Spieth was awarded the Knight's Cross on 24 March for his efforts, but there were several other crews who flew similar missions.

On 31 January 1943, Generaloberst Friedrich Paulus, commander of 6. *Armee* finally and momentously surrendered, along with German forces in the southern pocket. On 2 February, the remaining forces in

'*Lok-Töter*' Leutnant Udo Cordes of 9.(*Eis*)/KG 3 was a railway-attack specialist who accounted for the destruction of 81 enemy locomotives, as well as many trains, stations and bridges. He was awarded the Knights' Cross on 25 May 1943, and by the end of the war had flown 296 combat missions. He is standing here before his Ju 88C-6, which carries the *Geschwader* emblem of KG 3 along with winged railway wheel insignia of his *Staffel* (*John Weal*)

the northern pocket gave up the fight as well. With that, the strategic initiative in the East started to shift irrevocably away from Germany, but the Ju 88 soldiered on.

In January 1943, a new specialist railway attack *Staffel* in the form of the 9.(*Eis*)/KG 3 was raised under the leadership of Oberleutnant Ernst Fach. This '*Eisenbahn*' ('*Eis.*'/railway) *Staffel* comprised a small number of Ju 88C-6 *Zerstörer* that were tasked with attacking the Soviet rail network in the Donets Basin.

Fach had transferred to the Luftwaffe from the army in April 1933 and undertook bomber training. From the outbreak of war until May 1941, he flew Do 17s with 4./KG 3 in Poland, the West and over England, during which he became adept at making attacks on specific targets such as airfields. Converting to the Ju 88, Fach was assigned to 6./KG 3, and in the first months of *Barbarossa* he accounted for numerous tanks, artillery positions and bridges destroyed, as well as nine trains and an enemy fighter in air combat. His Ju 88A-4 was shot down into enemy territory on 26 March 1942, but Fach managed to return to German lines with his crew. He was appointed *Staffelkapitän* of 6./KG 3 shortly thereafter, and in August 1942 took command of 4. *Staffel*. Then, in January, he was given command of 9.(*Eis*)/KG 3.

In a matter of weeks, the Ju 88C-6s had destroyed 216 Russian railway engines (with Fach accounting for 44 of them) and damaged 40 more. In April 1943, having flown 300 combat missions, Fach was ordered not to fly further operations. By that time, his personal tally of locomotives had climbed to 64 and nine complete goods trains destroyed.

The *Staffel*'s airfield at Zaparozhye-East was bombed during April and one of its precious Ju 88s destroyed. A move to Poltava took place shortly afterwards. However, on 15 May 1943, while returning from a visit to the headquarters of *Luftflotte* 4, Fach's C-6 crashed near Poltava and he, together with his observer and radio operator were killed. He was awarded the Knight's Cross posthumously on 3 September 1943 and promoted to Hauptmann.

Fach's successor as *Kapitän* of 9.(*Eis*)/KG 3 was Dortmund-born Leutnant Udo Cordes, who developed a reputation as the *Lok-Töter* (locomotive-killer). Cordes joined II./KG 3 in the spring of 1942 and flew with both 4. and 6. *Staffeln* prior to being assigned to 9.(*Eis*)/KG 3 shortly after its establishment. In a period of three weeks, he and his crew destroyed 41 locomotives and 19 trains, including some single days where he accounted for several, such as 18 March when six engines and a fuel train were shot up by his C-6's guns. Cordes was awarded the Knight's Cross on 25 May 1943, by which time he had flown around 150 combat missions. In early 1944 he went on to serve as an instructor with the Royal Rumanian Air Force, returning to KG 3 in April of that year. In the penultimate month of the war, he was assigned to II./SG 2, flying Fw 190F-8s in ground-attack operations. Forced to bail out of his shot-up Focke-Wulf on 23 April 1945, Cordes survived this incident and was eventually captured by the Russians on 10 May, with whom he remained a prisoner until November 1949.

As the war on the Eastern Front slowly became defensive and the Luftwaffe's bomber units began a lingering retreat west, elsewhere the Ju 88 continued to shine as a combat aircraft.

CHAPTER FOUR

RANGING FAR AND WIDE

A side from having been employed as a dive-bomber, a *Schnellbomber*, a long-range night-intruder and a ground-strafer, the Ju 88 also performed an invaluable role as a fast, long-range reconnaissance aircraft.

Conceived as the Ju 88D, which was hoped would replace the Do 17P in the long-range reconnaissance role, the genesis of this series of aircraft lay in the extemporaneous works conversions of some standard A-models into which cameras were fitted in the rear bomb-bay, early examples being utilised by *Aufklärungsgruppe* (Aufkl.Gr) 121 and 122. The right-side bomb-bay door of a number of A-models were then fitted with two raised, circular, optical glazed camera panels, with a third in the left side, together with a debris deflection plate on the right. The forward part of the bay was converted to carry extra fuel. The aircraft would also have their dive-brakes and external bomb racks removed. In some cases, because of the urgent requirement for reconnaissance, in-the-field 'development' was undertaken at unit level.

The pre-production run of a dedicated reconnaissance variant, the D-0, commenced in 1940, with 1.(F)/122, based at Stavanger-Sola between April and June of that year, believed to have been the first unit to receive an example. The D-0 was followed by the D-2 series based on the Ju 88A-1 and A-5. First deliveries of the D-2 are believed to have gone to 1.(F)/123 in western France in the second half of 1940. To give this type

The engines are run up on Ju 88D-1 F6+DN of 5.(F)/122 on a cold day at Gosstkino in 1943 in readiness for another long-range reconnaissance mission over the Eastern Front. The aircraft has crudely-applied washable white paint over its uppersurfaces, but not the engine nacelles, which suggests the latter were recently replaced. The spinners are in the *Staffel* colour of red and the rear fuselage band is in the theatre colour of yellow (*Author's collection*)

Vital to keeping the Luftwaffe's Ju 88 bombers, nightfighters, *Zerstörer* and reconnaissance aircraft in the air, often in extremely adverse climatic or operating conditions, were the army of mechanics, electricians and armourers. Here, mechanics work on the left Jumo engine of a Ju 88A-1 or A-4 from an unidentified unit at a Luftwaffe repair and maintenance field (*Author's collection*)

increased performance – important for reconnaissance – the design was to be fitted with Jumo 211G or H engines, and underwing racks were carried for auxiliary fuel tanks.

A test machine in the form of the Ju 88 V21 was fitted with remotely-controlled Rb 50/30 high-altitude and/or Rb 20/30 low-altitude cameras. It also had petrol-fired heating equipment for the internal rear fuselage section, with an exhaust vent in a streamlined fairing on the dorsal spine. Finally, as per the preliminary models, additional fuel tanks were built into the forward bay area. This aircraft flew for the first time in November 1940 and trials proved generally successful. So fitted, the ensuing Ju 88D-1 series, the first of which was rebuilt from an A-4, was finished without provision to bomb.

Evaluation of the new variant commenced at Rechlin in April 1941, but the demand from battlefronts for a high-speed reconnaissance aircraft was great, and so three months later orders were issued for a run of 1350 D-1s, of which 855 were to be *Trop* variants for operations in the Mediterranean. The engines on these latter machines were equipped with sand filters, and there was also survival equipment for overwater and desert missions.

Delays with the 1350 hp Jumo 211J-1 or J-2 engines meant that 1100 hp Jumo B-2s or 1180 hp 211G-1 or H-1 powerplants would be fitted initially. The Ju 88D-1 was able to carry the same external stores as the A-4, including long-range drop tanks, and was fitted with Rb 50/30 and Rb 20/30 cameras in various combinations mounted in the fuselage immediately aft of the bomb-bay. The D-1 quickly became the most common reconnaissance variant.

D-series aircraft were delivered to many of the Luftwaffe's reconnaissance *Gruppen*, as well as several of its *Wettererkundungsstaffeln* (weather reconnaissance squadrons) serving on the Western Front, in the Balkans and in Russia. In the Mediterranean and North Africa, the D-1 and D-2 *Trop* sub-variants eventually became the D-3 and D-4, both with sand filters and survival equipment as standard. In all D-2 to D-4s, the camera windows were flush with the fuselage. Camera provision on the following D-5, the final production variant, was upgraded to carry one Rb 50/30 and one Rb 75/30 high-altitude camera. One D-5 assigned to 1.(F)/120 was modified for long-range flights from Stavanger-Sola to Iceland in 1940, the aircraft's *Bola* being removed and the multi-panel 'beetle eye' nose being replaced by a rounded clear plastic fairing.

As an example of their peripatetic existence, one of the many units that operated the Ju 88D in the reconnaissance role was 3.(F)/*Aufklärungsgruppe* 10 *'Tannenberg'*. The *Staffel's* parent *Gruppe* had been awarded the honour title in commemoration of the Battle of Tannenberg in August 1914, which saw a great victory for German forces over the Russians. 3.(F)/Aufkl. Gr.10, under the command of Major Horst Klinger, had been formed in

November 1938 from elements of 3./Aufkl.Gr.11 at Neuhausen in East Prussia, and equipped initially with Do 17Fs, which, in addition to a pair of cameras, could carry a 4500-kg bomb load and had increased fuel capacity.

At the beginning of 1942, the *Staffel* handed over its Do 17s and was briefly pulled back to Ohlau, in Silesia, from the Eastern Front, where it converted to the Ju 88D-1 under the command of Hauptmann Bruno Rainer. From late January 1942, 3.(F)/Aufkl. Gr.10 then returned to Russia,

Ju 88A-5s of 7./KG 30 lined up in the snow at Banak or Bardufoss in northern Norway on the 'Polar Front'. Under Hauptmann Erich Stoffregen, II./KG 30 carried out missions against Allied convoys bound for the Soviet Union from March 1942. The *Gruppe* remained in the area until it was relocated south, to Sicily, in November of that year. Stoffregen would be awarded the Knight's Cross on 23 August 1942 in recognition of his anti-convoy work, especially against the convoy PQ-17

having *Fernaufklarungs Gruppe* (FAGr) 4 (under Major Friedrich Alpers) as its parent unit and operating from Poltawa, in central Ukraine, until June. The *Staffel's* Ju 88s tended to fly from their bases at very low level and then climb to around 9000 m as the target was approached. Once the required photographs had been taken, they would immediately head for home, returning once more to low altitude. The crews of 3.(F)/Aufkl. Gr.10, each comprising pilot, observer/navigator, flight engineer/gunner and radio operator, became very experienced at these kinds of missions, and several pilots were awarded the *Ehrenpokal* honour goblet for 'For Special Achievement in the Air War'.

In August 1942, 3.(F)/Aufkl.Gr.10 moved to Kharkov and then south again to Mariupol. From the latter location it flew long-range missions on behalf of the army to targets in the Don River bend, obtaining photographs of the railway lines leading to Saratow, the fighting in the area around Stalingrad and as far east as Astrakhan and to the northern Caucasus. The dangers of such missions were highlighted when the Ju 88D of Oberleutnant Hugo Oechsle went missing in action from Tazinskaya in December. With the aforementioned Soviet counteroffensive, which commenced in November, the *Staffel* was forced to abandon its base at Tazinskaya on 21 December. The more fortunate members of the unit escaped in motor vehicles assigned to 3.(F)/Aufkl.Gr.10, while the rest resorted to a long march on foot as far as Rostov. All but three of the *Staffel's* eight Ju 88D-1s and D-5s were left behind.

From Rostov, Major Klinger, who had taken over command from Rainer in October, led his men on a long journey back to Gutenfeld, in East Prussia, where, in early 1943, they were to prepare for conversion to the new, but troublesome, He 177 long-range bomber.

Throughout the war, some 70 long-range reconnaissance pilots and observers were awarded the Knight's Cross. Typical of this group was Hauptmann Albert Scheidig of 1.(F)/Aufkl.Gr.122 who would frequently fly missions in a lone aircraft for up to 12 hours at a time, deep over enemy territory.

Albert Scheidig was born on 3 March 1915 in Weitramsdorf in Upper Franconia. As a Leutnant, he received the Iron Cross Second Class on

RIGHT
Knight's Cross-holder Hauptmann Albert Scheidig (left) and his crew from 1.(F)/122 are welcomed back from another sortie over the Mediterranean, which also happened to be the unit's 2000th mission involving contact with, or operations over, enemy territory. The officer presenting the bouquet to Scheidig is probably Oberst Fritz Koehler, the *Gruppenkommandeur* of *Aufklärungsgruppe* 122, who was awarded the Knight's Cross on 4 November 1941 and became a Generalmajor in August 1944 while assigned to the Luftwaffe Personnel Office (*Author's collection*)

The crew of a Ju 88D-1 from 1.(F)/122 parade on their arrival at Gerbini in Sicily in December 1941, while still wearing their parachute harnesses and lifejackets. The *Staffel* would operate briefly under II. *Fliegerkorps* until being transferred to the newly formed *Fliegerführer Afrika*, performing offensive sorties in addition to pure reconnaissance missions. The unit's large emblem of a stork flying over the red sweep of a camera lens adorns the aircraft's nose

21 March 1940, followed by the First Class award on 13 June while operating from Stavanger-Sola in Norway in the area of *Luftflotte* 5. As a result of his highly valued reconnaissance missions off the Norwegian coast, he was awarded the *Narvikschild* (Narvik Shield) on 30 January 1941. Between August 1940 and May 1941 Scheidig undertook 57 operational missions, many of them armed reconnaissance sorties along the south coast of England from the *Gruppe's* base at Vendeville, during which he also bombed six enemy ships totalling 33,500 GRT. On 14 April 1941, he managed to defend a convoy of German ships against British fighter attack, and on 7 May Scheidig was commended officially by *General der Flieger* Bruno Loerzer, commander of II. *Fliegerkorps,* for a 'brave attack on a convoy near the English coast'.

In June 1941 1.(F)/Aufkl.Gr.122 relocated to Warschau in readiness for Operation *Barbarossa*, and from the commencement of the invasion Scheidig was active, flying short- and longer-range missions. On 12 December of that year he received the *Deutsches Kreuz in Gold*, and that same month his *Staffel* left Schatalowka, in the Soviet Union, for Gerbini, on Sicily. Scheidig had flown 112 sorties over Russia, and he would record exactly the same number over the Mediterranean. Many of the latter were reconnaissance missions over Malta, including repeated flights over Valetta harbour in March 1942. Scheidig also photographed British convoys en route to North Africa and the Suez Canal. On one occasion he managed to sink a 6000-GRT freighter shortly before the vessel reached Valetta to discharge its precious cargo.

Scheidig also flew a dangerous lone mission to reconnoitre Algiers harbour. On another occasion he received personal good wishes from Generalfeldmarschall Kesselring for his sinking of a 3000-GRT merchant vessel.

Scheidig was awarded the Knight's Cross on 16 April 1942, having accumulated a total of 463 hours on reconnaissance missions over enemy-occupied areas. On 6 November of that year, Scheidig's Ju 88D-1 was posted as missing in action in the Mediterranean, but he later returned after it transpired his aircraft had run out of fuel and he had made an emergency landing while on a sortie to Oran, in Algeria. Although Scheidig and his crew were interned by the Vichy French authorities, they had soon managed to escape. On 1 January 1943 he was promoted to Hauptmann. After a period on the *Führer-Reserve* Ob.d.L. from 16 April 1943, he returned to 1.(F)/Aufkl.Gr.122 in September 1944 when the *Staffel* was based in Poland, but a month later Scheidig was reassigned to take command of 4./*Flugzeugüberführungsgeschwader* 1.

After flying on virtually every front as one of the Luftwaffe's most valuable aircraft, the Ju 88D was phased out in 1944.

ATLANTIC COMBAT

On the coast of western France, Ju 88Cs had been fighting another kind of war. The *Fliegerführer Atlantik* had been established in early 1941 at Lorient, in western France, as a tactical command to coordinate and oversee Luftwaffe maritime offensive and reconnaissance air operations. However, from the summer of that year, by far the bulk of the Luftwaffe was committed to the east for the invasion of the Soviet Union. This meant that Luftwaffe commands in the West found it increasingly difficult to carry out the tasks allotted to them over the Atlantic and the Bay of Biscay, including that of maritime reconnaissance, anti-shipping and minelaying operations.

By early 1942 the bulk of the *Fliegerführer Atlantik's* offensive capability rested in the Fw 200 Condor aircraft of KG 40. They had performed well against enemy shipping, but as a result of an increase in the defensive armament carried by Allied vessels, the low-level, lateral attacks mounted by Condors that had proved so successful earlier had become increasingly unsustainable, initially against convoys, but soon even against single vessels.

In terms of fast, long-range, heavily armed day fighters, (Z)./KG 30 had been redesignated as a nightfighter unit in July 1940, leaving just the Ju 88A bombers of Kü.Fl.Gr.106 to be deployed against convoys off the eastern coast of Britain. Even these operations eventually passed to the control of IX. *Fliegerkorps*. The *Fliegerführer Atlantik* was then confined to operations off the south and west coasts of England, but in May 1942 U-boat Command again requested assistance to provide cover for its vessels as they transited in and out of the Bay of Biscay, and to repulse enemy anti-submarine aircraft. For the rest of 1942 and into 1943, this became the main function of the *Fliegerführer Atlantik* and its small number of twin-engined fighters.

Between 10-19 June 1942, III./KG 40 at Bordeaux had taken delivery of four Ju 88C-6 *Zerstörer*, and at the end of the month a fifth machine arrived. After a series of unit redesignations and operational training provided by IV./KG 6 at Brétigny, some initial sorties took place to cover U-boats. In July the Chief of the Luftwaffe General Staff, Generaloberst Jeschonnek, admitted the need for more *Zerstörer*, and the order was issued to form a *Zerstörerstaffel* of 15 Ju 88s. This led to the establishment of 13. *Staffel* at Nantes in August, followed some weeks later by a 14. *Staffel*. On 13 August 1942, the *Luftwaffenführungsstab* ordered the establishment of a whole *Gruppe* of Ju 88s for operations over the Biscay under the jurisdiction of a new *Stab* V./KG 40.

RIGHT
Berliner Gerhard Korthals became *Kommandeur* of V./KG 40 on 1 July 1942. He was awarded the Knight's Cross on 2 October of that year, and was killed when his Ju 88C-6 suffered mechanical problems and crashed north of Lorient just a month later on 3 November. Seen here earlier in the war while assigned to 2./KGr 100 in Norway in 1940, he was succeeded, briefly, by Hauptmann Helmut Dargel (*Chris Goss*)

A Ju 88A arrives back at its base, having completed its (unidentified) unit's 2000th mission, possibly in France. The aircraft has been configured for either anti-shipping or ground-attack work. The 20 mm MG FF cannon appears to have been factory-installed, with the bombsight window blanked out. Note also what appears to be a MG 81Z mounted in the 'beetle's eye' glazing for additional offensive armament

As *Gruppenkommandeur*, Hauptmann Gerhard Korthals was already in place in July. Korthals' military career went back to the *Reichswehr*, and he had joined the Luftwaffe shortly after its formation. Following bomber training, he spent a year with I./KG 152 before being posted to the *Erprobungsstelle* Rechlin, where he specialised in signals. Korthals then joined 2./KGr 100, flying He 111s with that unit over Poland in the weeks following the outbreak of war. Missions over Norway ensued, during which he is believed to have sunk an enemy destroyer, before being assigned to 8./KG 51 as *Staffelkapitän*. Korthals undertook bombing missions against targets in England, the Balkans and Russia with the latter unit, gaining a reputation from his work attacking transport and bridge targets. He was officially appointed *Kommandeur* of the embryonic V./KG 40 on 1 July 1942.

The Ju 88C-6s quickly went into action, in mid-July, before the official establishment of V. *Gruppe*, and the unit's first kill is believed to have been credited to Feldwebel Henry Passier, who shot down a Wellington on 15 July. By the end of 1942, the *Gruppe* had registered 27 Allied aircraft shot down over the Biscay, from the north coast of Spain to Brest, and beyond to the coast of Cornwall, at a cost of eight Ju 88Cs destroyed and one badly damaged. Most of the unit's victims were Wellingtons or Whitleys, although the *Gruppe* also shot down a Sunderland, a Halifax, a Hudson, Beaufighters, a P-38, a P-39 and a B-17 in that period.

One of V./KG 40's prominent scorers was Leutnant Kurt Necesany of 13. *Staffel*. He was born in Ödenburg, in Hungary, on 28 November 1920, the son of a German mother and a Czech father. In 1939, Kurt took the nationality of his mother and joined the Luftwaffe in October of that year. He is believed to have served with KG 30 at one time, but transferred to 13./KG 40 at its formation. He lodged his first, shared, claim over a Wellington on 11 September, this aircraft probably being the No 311 'Czechoslovak' Sqn machine that engaged Ju 88s but managed to return to base. This went some way to avenge the death of his *Staffelkapitän*, Hauptmann Paul Heide, who had been killed while engaging a Whitley 48 hours earlier. Six days later, on the 17th, Necesany shot down a Hudson of No 500 Sqn over the Biscay and on the 24th he shared in the destruction of a Wellington, possibly from No 304 'Polish' Sqn, with Unteroffizier Heinz Scholz, also of 13./KG 40. On the 30th a Whitley of No 51 Sqn also fell to Necesany's guns.

In October, V./KG 40 claimed six RAF aircraft shot down for the loss of one Ju 88 that fell to Beaufighters. On the 16th, three Ju 88C-6s were out on patrol over the Biscay when another Whitley from No 51 Sqn emerged in the distance over the sea. Flying one of the Junkers, Leutnant Necesany led the three *Zerstörer* towards their prey and soon circled around it. Necesany went in first, opening fire as the Whitley stayed doggedly on course before pieces of the rudder flew away, forcing its pilot to adopt evasive manoeuvres. The Ju 88s attacked again and again, and on the sixth and final pass the enemy aircraft's right engine began to burn. According to a subsequent German report, Necesany had 'shot the Whitley to pieces', after which it crashed into the sea and five depth charges it was carrying exploded, spuming water into the air to a height of 70 m, while a film of oil gathered on the surface.

Flying alongside Necesany that day was future ace Leutnant Dieter Meister. Shortly after reforming, the German crews spotted a Wellington and a 15-minute pursuit over water ensued. The RAF bomber's Polish pilot was heading for the English coast and skilfully attempted to throw his attackers off, while his crew fired their machine guns effectively. As a means of gaining speed, the Wellington crew released their depth charges, but Meister closed in low and above, despite attracting fire from the rear gunner. Eventually, he was forced to pull back with one of his engines damaged and leaking coolant, and the kill was credited to his comrade, Unteroffizier Werner Steurich. Nevertheless, Meister returned home safely and was credited with Necesany for a shared victory over the Wellington.

It was not his first taste of victory, for on the afternoon of 8 October he had shot down a Whitley from No 10 OTU, and had three further shared kills. Born on 24 February 1919, Meister was a native of Hamburg, and along with Necesany he would become one of V./KG 40's most successful pilots.

Six days earlier Gerhard Korthals had earned recognition for his *Gruppe*'s activities with the award of the Knight's Cross on 2 October, but on 3 November he was killed in the crash of a C-6 after it developed mechanical problems while on a training flight off the western coast of France. Korthals had flown more than 300 combat missions by the time of his death. His place was taken by Hauptmann Helmut Dargel, but in a measure of the increasing attrition being experienced over the Biscay and the Atlantic, Dargel was lost on 30 December following an engagement with a USAAF P-39 southwest of Lorient. The Airacobra was one of 17 drawn from the 81st Fighter Group and 68th Observation Group that were being led by a B-25 from Predannack, in Cornwall, to North Africa via Gibraltar. One of the P-39s fell to Oberfeldwebel Georg Heuer of 14./KG 40 in return.

On 15 January 1943, the *Fliegerführer Atlantik* reported 35 Ju 88Cs on the strength of V./KG 40, of which 19 were serviceable, with two *Staffeln* at Kerlin-Bastard and one at Bordeaux-Merignac. The Junkers would primarily cover an area between 9°-11°W and 43°-45°N, although some missions went as far as 16°30'W. Sometimes, they would fly as escorts to surface ships and blockade-runners or damaged U-boats, although there was no direct contact with the latter because of technical shortcomings with radio equipment.

The *Kriegsmarine* desperately needed 'eyes' to search for convoys out in the Atlantic, but it simply did not have enough dedicated aircraft. In theory, when fitted with long-range auxiliary tanks, the Ju 88C *Zerstörer* would be able to reach 17°W as a stand-in reconnaissance aircraft. However, the main problem facing V./KG 40 was not a shortage of aircraft

Leutnant Kurt Necesany served as *Staffelkapitän* of 14./KG 40, later 2./ZG 1, then as Operations Officer of I./ZG 1. Born in Hungary to German and Czech parents, he is credited with six victories. Having inflicted mortal damage on a PB4Y-1 of VB-103 on 14 February 1944, his Ju 88C-6 was hit by return fire and it plunged into the waters of the Bay of Biscay (*Chris Goss*)

Hamburg-born Leutnant Dieter Meister joined 13./KG 40 in the early autumn of 1942. He became a proficient daylight *Zerstörer* pilot and was eventually posted to the single-seat fighter arm, serving with JG 2 as a *Staffelkapitän* until he was killed in combat with USAAF fighters in November 1944 (*Chris Goss*)

or equipment, but the supply of personnel. There was a grave lack of experienced *Zerstörer* pilots, which in turn meant that a number of aircraft were grounded because of insufficient crews.

For most of 1943, the *Zerstörer* would fly missions hunting for Allied aircraft as far as Cape Finisterre, in Spain, as well as intercepting the air transport route between Britain, Gibraltar and Portugal, although contact with the enemy was sporadic in the first weeks of the year because of inclement weather conditions. On 7 February 1943, the newly promoted Oberleutnant Necesany was appointed *Staffelkapitän* of 14./ KG 40 following the loss of Hauptmann Hans William Reicke, whose C-6 was shot down by Beaufighters on 30 January. Necesany would not score again until 14 May, when he shared in the destruction of a Sunderland from No 461 Sqn RAAF with Leutnant Willi Gutermann. He enjoyed further success on 18 July when he shot down a Liberator from No 53 Sqn and damaged another from No 224 Sqn. Necesany claimed yet another Liberator (again from No 224 Sqn) for his fifth victory on 4 October.

14. *Staffel* would gain some post-war notoriety when it was realised that the civilian KLM/BOAC-operated DC-3 inadvertently shot down in the early afternoon of 1 June by Oberleutnant Albrecht Bellstedt was the aircraft carrying the British actor Leslie Howard. For his part, Bellstedt would be credited with eight victories by war's end, the majority of these being claimed in a Ju 88C.

The summer of 1943 would see an increase in the intensity of combat operations, such as that on 11 June when five Ju 88s tangled with six Mosquito IIs flown by crews from Nos 25 and 264 Sqns. A swirling, low-level skirmish took place over the water which saw future ace Flt Lt Joe Singleton of No 25 Sqn shoot down the Ju 88 flown by Feldwebel Fritz Hiebsch of 15./KG 40. After this action, *Luftflotte* 3 noted ominously 'with a further increase in the numbers of Mosquitos we can reckon on further losses'.

On 13 October 1943, a wholesale redesignation of the *Gruppe* took place when 13., 14. and 15. *Staffeln* became 1., 2. and 3./ZG 1 and 16./KG 40 became 9./ZG 1.

Necesany retained command of 2./ZG 1 and was appointed *Gruppe* Operations Officer on 8 November 1943. By the middle of that month, 1. and 2./ZG 1 were at Lorient and 3./ZG 1 at Bordeaux-Mérignac with some 40 Ju 88Cs and Ju 88R-2s under Hauptmann Horst Grahl. 7./ZG 1 was also at Lorient with Ju 88Cs under Hauptmann Hans Morr. The R-2 was a progressive development of the C-6 introduced in mid-1943, the aircraft being powered by BMW 801MA or C engines that gave it a 50 km/h increase in speed over the Ju 88C.

For some days in mid-November, the Germans had been shadowing the Britain-bound convoy SL.139/MKS.30 from Freetown and Gibraltar. By the 20th, it was planned to attack the convoy with the U-boats of the *Schill* wolfpack that evening in a line 46°15'N 18°00'-21°30'W. *Fliegerführer Atlantik* would provide reconnaissance during the morning via Fw 200s from III./KG 40, which would be replaced by a single Ju 290 from FAGr.5 in the afternoon. Eight Ju 88s of 3./ZG 1 were despatched to offer cover to the lone Ju 290 'shadower', rendezvousing

Ju 88s of 14./KG 40 taxi out at an airfield in western France for another mission over the Bay of Biscay in the late summer of 1943. The aircraft in the foreground has been delivered in the unit's later grey, nightfighter style of camouflage, more suitable for overwater operations (*Chris Goss*)

with it as scheduled. During the afternoon, however, at a point off Cape Ortegal at the northwestern tip of Spain, the German formation was spotted by a patrol of four RAF Mosquito IIs from No 157 Sqn, led by Wg Cdr James A Mackie. According to No 157 Sqn's subsequent intelligence report, 'Course was set at "0" feet for 48°N 07°30'W. Cape Ortegal was sighted at 1351 hrs. The weather was murky – ten-tenths cloud at 1500-2000 ft, with visibility for two miles. The Mosquitos then clashed in a large aerial engagement, which also included Beaufighters of No 248 Sqn, 13 km off the Spanish coast'.

The Mosquitos first spotted the Ju 88s of ZG 1 two minutes after sighting Cape Ortegal, flying in two *Schwärme* of four aircraft that were in turn separated into two-aircraft *Rotten* strung out in line astern at 600 m, just below the cloud some 13 km north of Estaca Point. The Mosquitos made their attack in sections, but before they could get into range the Ju 88s climbed into the cloud. The RAF fighters gave pursuit, Mackie later reporting;

'The Ju 88s kept leaving and entering the cloud every few moments, singly and in pairs, and appeared to be flying in a wide circle. A running and rather confused dogfight ensued. Wg Cdr Mackie made five separate attacks on enemy aircraft, taking violent evasive action as they broke cloud. Four of the attacks were at extreme range, a short burst being given in each case – no results were observed. In the fifth attack, he gave a short burst from 300 yards and strikes were seen in the port wing root and on the fuselage just before the enemy aircraft went into cloud. This Ju 88 is claimed damaged. Inaccurate return fire was seen in each case.

'Flt Lt [George] Dyke gave a short burst at an enemy aircraft disappearing into cloud, and no strikes were seen. He saw two Ju 88s doing a climbing turn towards cloud; two short bursts from 300 to 400 yards were fired at the second one and strikes seen on the port wing root. The enemy aircraft peeled off and was lost. This Ju 88 is claimed as damaged. Almost at once another enemy aircraft was seen making for cloud. The Mosquito followed and opened fire from 400 yards, closing to 200 yards. Strikes were seen on the starboard engine and a piece flew off. The enemy aircraft disappeared into cloud, with black smoke pouring from its starboard engine. At this moment return fire splintered the windscreen of the Mosquito. This Ju 88 is claimed as probably destroyed.'

When Flt Lt Dyke returned to base it was found that his aircraft had been hit by machine gun fire in the starboard tank, twice in the port wing and twice on the propellers in addition to the windscreen.

Flg Off John Clifton also made four attacks on different Ju 88s at maximum range without effect, and in one of the attacks a Ju 88 turned to make a head-on pass at his Mosquito. On Clifton's fifth attempt he saw strikes hitting the port engine of his target and black smoke began to stream out. However, the only Ju 88C-6 and crew lost as a result of this engagement was that of Oberleutnant Hans Schuster, *Staffelkapitän* of 3./ZG 1. Schuster had received the *Ehrenpokal* on 1 November. His place at the head of the *Staffel* would be taken temporarily by Leutnant Alfred Klaus.

On 20 December, *Stab* and I./ZG 1 at Lorient reported 53 Ju 88Cs on strength with 36 ready, and 25 crews ready, while 7./ZG 1 at Bordeaux reported 16 Ju 88Cs with 11 ready, and seven crews.

On 14 February 1944, Necesany led a *Rotte* on a patrol over the Bay of Biscay, during which contact was made with a US Navy PB4Y-1 four-engined patrol bomber of VB-103. Necesany attacked and severely damaged the enemy aircraft (which later crashed), but his C-6 was also hit by defensive fire. He and his crew failed to return from the mission, and despite search attempts no trace was found of them. Kurt Necesany was credited with six victories, plus a number of shared destroyed and damaged claims.

As the Allies increased their air activity in the lead-up to the invasion of France, conditions became ever harder for the outnumbered *Zerstörer* crews at their bases at Lorient, Bordeaux-Mérignac, Vannes and Salon-de-Provence. On 6 June, the day of the Normandy landings, four Ju 88s were shot down and the next day six crews were lost. On 8 June, the *Gruppe* was consolidated at Nantes, but on the 11th it pulled back south to Cazeaux. The number of viable operations fell drastically, and on 5 August I. and III./ZG 1 were disbanded, with many of the pilots either being sent to II.(*Sturm*)/JG 4 for missions in defence of the Reich, or for the night-qualified crews of 9. *Staffel*, to 1./NJG 4. Oberleutnant Dieter Meister was posted as *Staffelkapitän* of Fw 190-equipped 10./JG 2, but he was killed during combat with either P-38s or P-51s on 21 November 1944.

Away to the south, and based initially at Trapani in Sicily, for much of 1943 another *Staffel* of Ju 88C-6 *Zerstörer* performed a different kind of mission. The C-6s of 10./ZG 26, which had reformed in April 1942 initially on Bf 110s, possibly at Derna, flew coastal patrols around southeast Europe and escorted Luftwaffe transports. From July 1943, however, the unit was occupied with ground-attack missions against American forces as they fought their way across Sicily. In June 1943, the *Staffel* relocated to Pratica de Mare, between Rome and Anzio, from where it carried out ground-attack missions in support of the German invasion of the Dodecanese Islands in September 1943. It was not long, however, until the unit was pulled back to Germany and redesignated 7./ZG 76.

CHAPTER FIVE

AFRICA AND THE MEDITERRANEAN

The first bomber unit to operate the Ju 88 in the Mediterranean theatre was LG 1. The *Geschwader* had deployed the Junkers over Norway in 1940 (see Chapter 1), but elements of the *Geschwaderstab* moved south from Lechfeld to Catania in December 1940 in preparation for the arrival of II. and III. *Gruppen* there the following month, where they would operate as part of the Luftwaffe's Mediterranean strike force, X. *Fliegerkorps*. From January 1941, II. and III./LG 1 flew regular sorties to Malta, where they attacked airfields and warships in the harbour. The calibre of its crews was high, with further operational experience being gained by I./LG 1 during the campaign in the Balkans.

Amongst the combat veterans assigned to the unit was Hauptmann Horst Beeger, *Staffelkapitän* of 3./LG 1. Born on 8 June 1913 in the east Saxony town of Bautzen, Beeger had served as an artilleryman in the *Wehrmacht* until 1936, when he joined the Luftwaffe for bomber training. After a period with the *Lehrgeschwader 'Greifswald'*, which became LG 1 in November 1938, he had transferred to the *Geschwaderstab* headquarters by the time Germany invaded Poland. Beeger soon undertook operations in the He 111, prior to converting to the Ju 88 in time to fly missions over

Ju 88C-6 F1+KT of Hauptmann Dieter Lukesch, *Staffelkapitän* of 9./KG 76, at Catania, Sicily, in May 1943. This was one of a small number of C-6s operated by the *Gruppe* in 1942-43 and it is finished in a rarely seen, close scribble camouflage pattern together with the white Mediterranean theatre fuselage band

A typical scene at an airfield in North Africa as a pilot carrying his map case walks past bombs toward Ju 88A-4 L1+MA of the *Geschwader Stab* of LG 1. Note the heavy exhaust staining on the sand-coloured outer nacelle of the port Jumo 211 engine

Knight's Cross-holder Hauptmann Horst Beeger commanded 3./LG 1 from 1 October 1940 to 19 August 1942 – a time when the *Staffel* sank around 20 merchant vessels. After accomplished service in the Mediterranean, Beeger was transferred to France, where he took over operational training unit III./KG 101. Subsequently being posted to the staff of the *General der Kampfflieger*, he ended the war overseeing the coordination of the Luftwaffe's air-launched flying bomb campaign against the British Isles (*Author's collection*)

Norway and the West. Taking part in regular bombing attacks on England and enemy shipping in the English Channel, he was appointed to lead 3. *Staffel* on 10 October 1940.

Beeger flew a number of missions during the campaign in the Balkans, and on one occasion he and his crew survived a forced-landing in enemy territory in Greece to return safely to German lines. He would really demonstrate his forte as a bomber pilot in the Mediterranean, initially against enemy warships off Crete but also over Malta. Beeger was awarded the Knight's Cross on 23 November 1941 while an Oberleutnant. By that time, his *Staffel* had accounted for the sinking of 17 enemy merchant vessels in Mediterranean waters, and Beeger had also led his Ju 88s on mining missions to the Suez Canal and over North Africa. In April 1942 he was posted to a unit leader's course in France and then took over the operational training unit III./KG 101 at Cognac. Later assignments took Beeger to the staff of the *General der Kampfflieger*, and then in the autumn of 1944 to the *Stab* of KG 53, which was engaged in air-launching V1 flying bombs from its He 111s against the British Isles. He ended the war on the staff of KG 200.

One of Beeger's pilots in 3./LG 1 was Oberfeldwebel Heinrich Boecker from Spenge, to the north of Bielefeld. A former policeman, he joined the Luftwaffe in 1935 and embarked on fighter training with I./JG 137, but requested a transfer to the bomber arm. Like Beeger, Boecker joined the *Lehrgeschwader 'Greifswald'* and flew in the Polish campaign assigned to the *Stabsstaffel* of LG 1. Flying with Beeger throughout the Western, Channel and Balkan campaigns, Boecker eventually arrived in the Mediterranean and undertook several early sorties against British warships off Greece from the *Staffel's* base at Plovdiv-Krumovo. Transferring with I./LG 1 on 20 May to Eleusis in Greece, he commenced operations against Crete that afternoon, when I./LG 1 made two attacks in close formation against ships in Souda Bay – the first through dense anti-aircraft fire. In his Ju 88A-5, Boecker managed to score a direct hit on a 6000-GRT cargo vessel with SC-500 and SC-1000 bombs. The ship sank a short time later.

Twice in 1941 Boecker would go on to have lucky escapes. During the evening of 22 May, while leading a *Kette* of Ju 88s from 3./LG 1 to attack British ships, his aircraft was hit by anti-aircraft fire near Kythira Island. Boecker had attempted to attack the cruiser HMS *Fiji* while it was trying to render assistance to the crew of the mortally damaged destroyer HMS *Greyhound*, which had already been badly holed by German bombing. The captain of *Fiji* had reluctantly decided to leave *Greyhound* and steam south with two destroyers after more enemy bombers were spotted nearby. The vessel was eventually targeted 20 times, and had fired almost every round of its anti-aircraft ammunition when Boecker commenced his attack.

Although *Fiji* would also be sunk later that evening (by Leutnant Gerhard Brenner of 2./LG 1), in the process of making his bombing run Boecker's Ju 88 was hit in the radiator for its right engine. His bombs fell some 50 m astern of *Fiji* as the vessel started to zigzag on an evasive course. Meanwhile, with the bomber's oil and water temperatures climbing rapidly, Boecker ordered his radio operator to jettison the cabin hood as the Ju 88 descended to a height of 20 m. Moments later, while still travelling at a speed of 170 km/h, the bomber ditched into the sea. Although the cabin quickly filled with water, Boecker and his crew managed to clamber into their emergency dinghy somewhere northwest of Crete. They were fortunate to be picked up by friendly Greek fisherman and returned to their unit.

A few weeks later, on 6 August 1941, having been promoted to Oberleutnant, Boecker flew a night-bombing sortie to Egypt. En route to the target his Ju 88A-5 suffered a fuel pump failure and he was forced to land on the southern coast of Turkey, from where he and his crew were subsequently interned in Ankara. In January 1942 Boecker was able to escape by concealing himself in a consignment of wool. He managed to make it to Bulgaria and eventually rejoined LG 1 in April 1942, taking command of 12(*Erg.*) *Staffel*. Boecker then flew several missions over North Africa before eventually returning to the Reich, where he took command of a training school.

Amongst other things, he trained pilots to fly anti-tank missions in *Panzerfaust*-armed Bü 181s, as well as being involved with the notorious *Schulungslehrgang Elbe* – the command intended to carry out a mass ramming operation by single-engined fighters against enemy daylight bombers in the final weeks of the war. Hauptmann Heinrich Boecker was awarded the Knight's Cross on 29 February 1944, having flown 185 combat missions, many of which were long-range over the Mediterranean and North Africa.

For most of the campaign in the Mediterranean, many Ju 88 pilots continued to execute diving attacks on enemy ships. This usually involved an approach flight of between 3000 and 5000 m. The pilot would look through a small window in the floor of the aircraft to observe the target and then level out using the artificial horizon. Etched on the floor window was a series of parallel lines perpendicular to the line of flight to enable calculation of distance to the target. Prior to diving, the direction and strength of the wind would need to be checked, so the navigator would look for any smoke emanating from a ship's funnel and then the pilot would call out for final checks – throttles back, propellers set to coarse pitch to prevent the engines over-speeding in the dive and the BZA dive-bombing sight switched on.

Hauptmann Joachim Helbig (right) was a leading Ju 88 pilot and tactician. Having flown in the Norwegian campaign, he was appointed *Kommandeur* of I./LG 1 on 5 November 1941, and held that position until 24 January 1943 when he was assigned as an inspector of the staff of the *General der Kampfflieger*. Helbig had sunk 22,000 GRT of shipping, with another 11,000 GRT damaged, by the time he was awarded the Knight's Cross on 24 November 1940. He then led I./LG 1 through the early years of the Mediterranean campaign, seeing action over Crete and North Africa. Helbig was awarded the Oak Leaves on 16 January 1942, having flown 210 missions over enemy territory and against shipping. He received the Swords eight months later. Returning to LG 1 as its *Kommodore* in August 1943, he actively led the *Geschwader* as the Allies landed at Salerno and then Anzio-Nettuno. During the last year of the war, Helbig led a composite air battle group in offensive operations over northwest Europe, being wounded in an Allied air attack in mid-September 1944. Upon his recovery, he returned to operations, ending the war with 350 missions over the West and the Mediterranean. He is seen here in front of his Ju 88 L1+MH, armed with an MG/FF cannon, at Iraklion, on Crete, in the summer of 1942

As the target vessel passed under the last of the lines in the window, the pilot would extend the underwing dive brakes, causing a nose-down trim change, lifting the tail and tilting the aircraft into its 60-degree dive. The target would now appear on the reflector glass of the BZA sight directly in front of the pilot. Holding his aircraft steady in the dive, with increasing speed, often with enemy tracer passing around it or flak exploding close by, required skill, stamina and calm nerves.

From 3000 m the dive lasted 15 seconds, at the end of which the Ju 88 would be travelling at around 580 km/h. At 1500 m from the pre-set target altitude a horn would sound to prepare the pilot for bomb release. Four seconds later, at 1000 m, the bomb-release horn would sound, at which point the pilot would press the button on his control column. As the bombs were released, the elevators were automatically reset in the 'up' position. The Junkers' nose pulled up and the aircraft recovered from its dive. The pilot retracted the dive brakes, selected fine pitch on the propellers and opened the throttles. It was at this point that the aircraft was most vulnerable to defensive fire from the target ship.

TURNING POINT

The year 1942 epitomised the peak of German military ambition and accomplishment, but it also saw the first cracks begin to appear in the scale of that accomplishment. By the spring of that year, the *Wehrmacht* had conquered vast areas of territory, with German troops serving from Kirkenes in northern Norway and the southern shores of Lake Ladoga in northern Russia to the Greek Islands and Gazala in Libya, while to the west they had occupied the Channel Islands and the French Atlantic coast. And all this within a year of invading the Soviet Union.

In the Western Desert on 21 January 1942, Rommel had launched a three-pronged advance towards Agedabia, which took him to Benghazi and on towards Gazala, before which he briefly halted on 6 February. From then on, the newly-named *Panzerarmee Afrika* pushed eastward, Rommel using his armour in a series of fast, sweeping manoeuvres, deflecting British counter-attacks, driving through minefields and eventually taking Tobruk on 21 June. By 1 July, German forces were at El Alamein.

The Luftwaffe's Ju 88 units supporting Axis forces in the Mediterranean were marshalled under *Luftflotte* 2, and on 27 July 1942 they comprised *Stab*, I. and II./LG 1 at Eleusis and Iraklion, *Stab* and I./KG 54 at Gerbini, *Stab*, II. and III./KG 77 at Gerbini and Comiso, KGr.606 and 806 at Catania and the torpedo-bombers of III./KG 26 at Grosseto, in Tuscany. Altogether, these units numbered 207 aircraft.

Another eminent and extremely experienced pilot and commander to serve with LG 1 in this theatre in 1941-42 was Hauptmann Karl Heinz Schomann from Lübeck, whose earlier wartime career has been recounted in Chapter 1. Assigned as a technical officer with the *Geschwaderstab* when LG 1 relocated to Sicily, he subsequently flew in attacks against Crete and Malta, North Africa and the Suez Canal. During the morning and afternoon of 26 March 1941, II. and III./LG 1 flew missions against a British convoy off Crete. At 1232 hrs, Ju 88s of II. *Gruppe* left Catania led by *Kommandeur* Hauptmann Gerhard Kollewe and located the reported

After a long period with KG 30 in the Mediterranean, during which time he had carried out many attacks on Malta, Crete, Tobruk and the Tunisian coast, Helmut Weinreich, a Prussian, was appointed *Kommandeur* of I./KG 30 based in the Far North. He was awarded the Knight's Cross on 22 January 1943 as an Oberleutnant, and is seen here as a Hauptmann with the award, and also the mission clasp with pendant for 400 missions. Weinreich later converted to flying single-engined nightfighters and was appointed *Kommodore* of JG 301 on 1 October 1943. He was killed a few weeks later on 18 November when his Fw 190 was hit by defensive fire as he shot down an enemy bomber (*Author's collection*)

convoy southwest of the island. The then Oberleutnant Schomann was flying with the formation and released three SC-250 bombs close to the side of the largest freighter in the convoy. As he turned away from the ship, there was a large explosion, from which bellowed white smoke. Schomann returned to Catania at 1816 hrs and a short while later was credited with the sinking of an 8000-GRT vessel.

He was promoted to Hauptmann on 1 April 1942 by which time he was responsible for all training in the *Geschwader*, but in early July he return to operations as *Staffelkapitän* of 5./LG 1 and flew bombing missions against Suez, Haifa and El Alamein. Schomann was wounded in action while flying a Ju 88A-4 on 8 December 1942, and after a period of recuperation he was appointed *Kommandeur* of II./LG 1 on 24 March 1943. Promoted to Major, he was transferred to take command of IV. *Gruppe* in October 1943, and on the 29th of that month was awarded the Knight's Cross in recognition of his combat record in the Mediterranean.

In July 1944 Schomann joined the staff of the *General der Kampfflieger* and became involved in organising training for the Me 262 and Ar 234 jet units. At the end of the war, he was serving with III./KG 51. Schomann is credited with completing 265 combat missions and sinking 32,000 GRT of enemy shipping in the waters off Norway and France and in the Mediterranean.

II./KG 77, under Knight's Cross-holder Hauptmann Heinrich Paepcke, had arrived in Comiso from Ansbach in January 1942 to share the airfield with III. *Gruppe*, which had arrived from Kitzingen after both units had enjoyed a period of rest and refitting on the Ju 88A-4 following combat in Russia. Until the spring both *Gruppen* were heavily involved in attacks on Malta, after which they relocated to Rennes and Vannes, respectively, for another period of rest, refit, training and some night raids against targets in England. However, the units were back in the Mediterranean from July, operating from Gerbini and Comiso.

On 10 August 1942, a heavily escorted Allied convoy carrying 32,000 tons of supplies entered the Mediterranean. The Luftwaffe promptly assembled some 130 Ju 88s drawn from I. and II./LG 1, I./KG 54, II. and III./KG 77 and KGr.606 and 806, in addition to which was added a large force of Italian long-range torpedo-bombers and Ju 87 dive-bombers to deal with it. The armada battled its way through to Malta under the codename Operation *Pedestal*, which saw significant casualties, including the loss of a Royal Navy aircraft carrier, two cruisers and a destroyer, plus several freighters, with other naval and merchant vessels damaged. Hauptmann Heinrich Paepcke, leading a formation of Ju 88s from KG 77, is credited with the sinking of a 12,000-GRT freighter on 12 August.

Paepcke would go on to fly missions in support of Rommel's offensive at El Alamein, as well as carrying out attacks on Alexandria and the Suez Canal. However, while undertaking a bombing raid on Malta on 17 October 1942, his Ju 88A-4 was struck head-on by the No 126 Sqn Spitfire V flown by American Flt Lt 'Rip' Jones and the aircraft plunged into the sea. Both pilots were killed, although Paepcke's crew was able to bail out safely. Paepcke's loss signalled the beginning of a gradually increasing and worrying climb in the numbers of experienced unit

One of the most experienced bomber pilots in the Luftwaffe, Oberstleutnant Hermann Hogeback is seen here as a Major and wearing the Oak Leaves to the Knight's Cross that he received on 19 February 1943. Hogeback was a successful anti-shipping pilot, flying in the Mediterranean with the Ju 88-equipped III./LG 1, of which he was appointed *Kommandeur* in early December 1941. He subsequently went to Russia, leading his *Gruppe*'s Ju 88s in gruelling combat over Sevastopol, against enemy shipping on the Black Sea and in the advance on Stalingrad. Still flying the Ju 88, Hogeback then flew raids against targets in Britain in Operation *Steinbock* in early 1944, before switching to the Me 262. In mid-April 1945, as *Gefechtsverband Hogeback*, he commanded several Me 262 units in operations over the Prague area. He flew more than 500 combat missions during the war, becoming a recipient of the Swords to the Knight's Cross on 26 January 1945

A stellar line-up of Ju 88 bomber aces from KG 6 photographed in the summer of 1943. They are, from left to right, Hauptmann Rudolf Puchinger, *Staffelkapitän* of 8./KG 6, *Oberstleutnant* Walter Storp, *Geschwaderkommodore* of KG 6, and Major Hermann Hogeback, *Gruppenkommandeur* of III./KG 6. Although Ju 88-equipped KG 6 saw most of its action in northwest Europe, these three pilots had accumulated much of their considerable operational experience in the Mediterranean. Puchinger had flown successful anti-shipping missions against Malta and over the western Mediterranean with 8./LG 1, while Storp led elements of KG 6 in the defence of Sicily and Hogeback served twice in the Mediterranean, firstly with III./LG 1 and then taking over KG 6 from Storp. Between them, the three airmen had probably flown more than 1000 missions (*Author's collection*)

Heinrich Paepcke was a veteran anti-shipping ace who was amongst the first group of pilots to train on the Ju 88 after the outbreak of war. He commanded 7./KG 30 over Norway and in the West, accounting for four cruisers, three destroyers, a minelayer, a patrol boat and various merchantmen. Furthermore, he and his crew claimed the shooting down of five enemy fighters, and Paepcke was awarded the Knight's Cross on 5 September 1940. In 1942, he took command of II./KG 77 in the Mediterranean, but on 17 October he was killed when a Spitfire V collided with his Ju 88 head-on. Paepcke was posthumously awarded the Oak Leaves with the rank of Hauptmann (thus this propaganda photograph has been touched up)

commanders killed on operations in Russia and the Mediterranean. He is credited with around 125 missions and the destruction of two enemy aircraft in air combat.

Throughout 1942-43, the crews of KG 77 earned for themselves a reputation as anti-shipping bomber specialists. The *Geschwader's* I. *Gruppe* was reformed in September 1942 by the redesignation of Hauptmann Rolf Siedschlag's KGr.606 whose Ju 88s had been operating from Catania against Malta since December 1941. Two of the *Kampfgruppe's* notable pilots at the time of its redesignation were Leutnante Johannes Geismann and Karl-Heinz Greve. Both men were 23 years of age when they were awarded the Knight's Cross in late 1942.

Greve, from Münster in Westphalia, had joined the Luftwaffe in November 1939, and after undergoing standard bomber pilot training was assigned to 3./Kü.Fl.Gr.606 at Lannion, on France's Atlantic coast, in August 1941. The *Staffel* was equipped with Do 17Zs, although it was in the process of converting to the Ju 88. Appointed the *Staffel* Technical Officer, Greve gained operational experience from attacking shipping off the southern coast of England and in British ports. Transferring with his *Gruppe* to Sicily, Greve commenced a successful period of operations striking at enemy shipping in the Mediterranean, especially around Malta. On 7 October 1942 he was awarded the Knight's Cross in recognition of his destruction of six merchant vessels totalling 51,000 GRT, as well as, reportedly, two submarines and a destroyer, plus damage inflicted on an aircraft carrier, a cruiser and a tanker.

Johannes Geismann was born at Hattingen in the Ruhr, and he followed a service career parallel to Greve, also joining the Luftwaffe in November 1939. Following completion of training, he was posted to 1./Kü.Fl.Gr.606 in the summer of 1941 which was also based at Lannion with Dorniers and Junkers. As with Greve, and now flying Ju 88s, Geismann enjoyed considerable success against Allied shipping around Malta.

These pilots' impressive records would continue when KGr.606 became I./KG 77, still under Siedschlag's command. Greve had by then risen to the rank of Hauptmann, and in early August 1943 he took over II./KG 77.

By this stage of the war, the *Gruppe* was committed to attacking enemy shipping off North Africa and Sicily. He claimed the sinking of three more merchantmen of 18,000 GRT and damage to a 4,000-GRT steamer prior to II./KG 77 being transferred to East Prussia at the end of September for torpedo training.

Geismann's Knight's Cross came on 21 December 1942 after he had sunk a 20,000-GRT passenger ship and a transport of 7000 GRT in the harbour at Bougie, in Algeria, on 12 November. Prior to that he was credited with 71,000 GRT of enemy shipping sunk or damaged, much of it claimed during night raids against ports in French North Africa. Geismann's I./KG 77 preceded II. *Gruppe* in its return to the Reich for torpedo training by one month.

Pressure came on Axis forces in North Africa when the British Eighth Army broke through Rommel's defences on 2 November and Tobruk was abandoned – events which immediately followed a month of ever-dwindling fuel supply for the (renamed) *Deutsch-Italienische Panzerarmee* as it fought to hold on to Cyrenaica. Even as the Germans pulled back towards Tunisia, pursued by the Eighth Army, the Allies had landed in northwest Africa in Operation *Torch*, opening up a second front in North Africa. The Germans duly decided to establish a bridgehead at Tunis.

In response to *Torch*, the Luftwaffe frantically turned to its long-range bomber units, rushing them in from Germany and other parts of the Mediterranean to attack the concentration of shipping off the Algerian coast and to dismember the landings.

The Ju 88 was first outfitted to carry torpedoes in numbers during the first half of 1942. Development had commenced the previous year with the V46, and led to the Ju 88A-4 LT (*Luft Torpedo* – aerial torpedo) sub-variant. This differed from a standard A-4 principally in the replacement of the two external underwing ETC bomb racks inboard of the engines with PVC torpedo racks and a dedicated torpedo sight in the cockpit, from which it was possible to input the torpedo run control settings. The necessary control mechanism was housed in a fairing that extended from the nose of the aircraft back towards the wing and the racks. The latter, which were larger and deeper than the ETC racks, were able to carry one LT F5b torpedo each.

Groundcrew haul a laden bomb trolley across the grass prior to loading a 1000-kg device onto the underwing rack of a Ju 88A, probably of KG 77, for an anti-shipping sortie from an Italian airfield in late 1943/early 1944 (*Author's collection*)

RIGHT
Ten ship sinkings were claimed by the crew of Ju 88A-4 Wk.-Nr1016 3Z+DB, led by Leutnant Johannes Geismann (seen here) of I./KG 77 based at Catania, on Sicily, for the first nine months of 1942. When Kü.Fl.Gr 606 was redesignated as I./KG 77 in September 1942, Geismann commenced flying operations over North Africa. He was awarded the Knight's Cross on 21 December 1943 and would eventually be credited with the sinking or damaging of 71,000 GRT of shipping. He flew a number of torpedo-bombing missions before KG 77 was disbanded and later retrained as a nightfighter pilot. By the end of the war he commanded a *Staffel* within IV./NJG 1. Close examination of the photograph reveals the small emblem at the top of the tailplane depicting a cartoon cockerel, so used in recognition of the former commander of Kü.Fl.Gr 606, Major Joachim Hahn – 'Hahn' being the German word for cockerel

Hauptmann Erich Stoffregen, *Kommandeur* of II./KG 30, returns to Comiso, on Sicily, at the end of November 1942 after completing his 150th combat mission. Stoffregen had received the Knight's Cross on 13 August of that year for missions conducted against Arctic convoys. Just a few weeks later, on 14 January 1943, together with a technician, he was killed in a flying accident while flight-testing a newly delivered Ju 88A-4 from Comiso

The LT F5b was powered by compressed air. Weighing 765 kg, it had a charge of 250 kg, was five metres in length and required a minimum depth of water of 16-20 m. Its range was 3000 m and speed was 33 knots. The torpedo's gyro would start to run as it was launched from the carrier aircraft, and the engine was started by the pressure from the water pushing back a flap as it went below the surface.

A second type was the Italian-manufactured F5W 'Whitehead' torpedo, which was also powered by compressed air, weighed 900 kg and had a charge of 195 kg. Slightly longer than the F5b, it had a speed of 36 knots. The 'Whitehead' torpedo was generally considered to have been the better of the two weapons mainly because of its sensitivity. The F5b's main weakness was that when hitting a target at more acute angles detonation was not always guaranteed, whereas the F5W, while not without faults, was generally satisfactory, although crews were encouraged to watch the track of a torpedo to make sure it was running properly. Unlike the F5b, however, it had no stabilising fins and a much more complex air rudder system.

Initial operations with the Ju 88A-4 LT were considered sufficiently successful to justify a small run of production variants, designated Ju 88A-17s, in which the most significant feature was the removal of the ventral gondola. The torpedo load was the same as for the A-4 LT.

As previously mentioned, the first Ju 88 unit to receive training and equipment for torpedo operations was III./KG 26 based at Banak, in Norway, under Hauptmann Ernst Thomsen, where the unit had converted to the Junkers from the He 111 in June 1942. Training was provided at *Kampfschulgeschwader* (KSG) 2 at Grosseto. KSG 2 had originally been established in October 1941 at Grossenbrode from the *Stab* of the *Torpedoschule und Erprobungsstelle der Luftwaffe*, but the airfield's location on the Baltic coast meant that the winter weather, which frequently brought snow and ice, hampered training efforts, and so a decision was made to move the school to Grosseto.

When the Allies landed in North Africa in November 1942, III./KG 26 immediately went into action from Grosseto, attacking Allied shipping around Algiers on the first day on the landings. During the evening of 8 November, 13 bomb- and torpedo-carrying Ju 88s led by Hauptmann Klaus-Wilhelm Nocken launched a strike on Allied warships, but lost three of their number in the process. The British destroyer HMS *Cowdray* was seriously damaged east of Cape Natifou. Torpedoes missed the vessel, but a bomb struck the forward structure on the starboard side and exploded under the hull. *Cowdray* suffered 17 casualties, including five that were fatal. The 9135-GRT combat-loaded USS *Leedstown* (AP-73) – a passenger/cargo ocean liner – was hit by a torpedo during the attack, demolishing its stern, shortly after the vessel had landed troops and supplies ashore east of Algiers. It was then sunk by bomb near-misses and hits from two more torpedoes.

It was the start of a protracted campaign for KG 26 in the Mediterranean, and Nocken continued to lead such torpedo attacks until early 1944.

Born in Krefeld on 20 November 1916, Nocken had joined the Luftwaffe in 1939 and started his operational flying with 1./Kü.Fl.Gr.906, equipped with He 59s and He 115s. He flew both seaplane types on reconnaissance and minelaying sorties around the British coast and in the North Sea. Appointed *Staffelkapitän* of 2./KSG 2 at Grosseto, he was deeply involved in devising torpedo training. Initially, Nocken's *Gruppe*, having converted to the Ju 88 from the He 111, flew missions against the Murmansk convoys from Banak in Norway. Having sunk a 9000-GRT freighter steaming with convoy PQ-18, Nocken led his unit to the Mediterranean.

On 9 November 1942, he was attacked by British fighters off Algiers and forced to ditch his Ju 88A-4 LT in the sea. Nocken and his radio operator were both wounded, but managed to survive for several hours in their dinghy, although the Junkers' observer and a war reporter are still listed as missing. Nocken and the radio operator were later rescued by a German U-boat. He was appointed *Kommandeur* of III./KG 26 at Grosseto on 20 December 1942 and was awarded the Knight's Cross on 29 October 1943 in recognition of his tactical leadership, especially in the field of torpedo operations.

Ju 88 torpedo operations would continue doggedly with both successes and losses as the Luftwaffe entered its final, critical last full year of war.

A Ju 88/A-4 LT loaded with a pair of F5b torpedoes. This interim variant retained the ventral gondola and, as seen here, the torpedo control mechanism was housed in a fairing which extended from the nose, adjacent to the control area in the cabin, back towards the wing leading edge and the underwing PVC rack. The air rudder at the rear of the torpedo would be released when it entered the water, but remained in place long enough to prevent the weapon from rolling while the engine started up and gathered speed

Newly arrived Ju 88s of an unknown unit at an Italian airfield. A generator cart has been plugged in to the aircraft in the foreground and the starboard engine has just fired up (*Author's collection*)

CHAPTER SIX

DAY AND NIGHT

A Ju 88A-14 of an unidentified unit is loaded up with aerial mines, possibly for deployment against Allied shipping off the coast of northwest France in mid-1944

In 1943, the *General der Kampfflieger* issued a sobering report on the comparative status of the Ju 88;

'The present Ju 88 is to be regarded as no longer fit for service by day in the Anglo-American theatre by reason of the extremely heavy losses: speed, armament and endurance are inadequate to cope with the enemy fighters and their escort system. For the time being it is serviceable for nightfighting if we discard two bomb racks and any speed-reducing armament and equip them with airborne interception aids. On the Eastern Front it can be used in good weather by day, and at night, when the losses are not unreasonably high.'

With the benefit of hindsight, this can be said to have been an accurate prognosis. Nevertheless, the Ju 88 did continue to demonstrate its multi-role capability well into 1944 through its employment as a torpedo-bomber. On 11 November 1943, II./KG 26, under Hauptmann Jochen Müller, was training up for torpedo operations at Lübeck/Blankensee and Grossenbrode with 16 (seven serviceable) Ju 88s and 46 crews, while the combat-seasoned III. *Gruppe* was at Montpellier with 34 (26) Ju 88s and 25 crews.

The following day, Hauptmann Günther Trost, at that time *Staffelkapitän* of the training unit 12./KG 26, was awarded the Knight's Cross for his accomplishments as a *Torpedoflieger*. Tröst had flown with the reformed III./KG 26 since June 1942, undertaking missions against the Murmansk

convoys from Banak. Relocating to
Grosseto in early November, Tröst
and his *Gruppe* flew many missions
against Allied convoys off North
Africa, but such were his capabilities
that he was assigned for a period to
the staff of the *Bevollmächtigten für
die Lufttorpedowaffe* (Plenipotentiary
for the Aerial Torpedo Arm). He
carried out 42 combat missions
against enemy shipping in the North
Sea and Atlantic and 47 against
convoys in the Mediterranean.

A Ju 88A-4 at the torpedo test centre at
Gotenhafen-Hexengrund loaded with two
experimental Blohm und Voss L 10 glider
torpedo carriers fitted to standard LT F5b
practice torpedoes. The latter are fitted with
red and white dummy heads

Stab/KG 77 was based at
Königsberg under Eastern Front
veteran and future Knight's
Cross-holder Major Wilhelm Stemmler, with I. *Gruppe* at Grieslinen
and II./KG 77 at Wormditt with just 15 aircraft. These units were
also undergoing torpedo training, having returned, battered, from the
Mediterranean in September 1943.

When the Allied landings took place at Anzio and Nettuno in late January
1944, Hauptmann Nocken's III./KG 26 was moved from Montpellier to
Piacenza to be closer to launch attacks on the enemy beachhead, but the
supply of torpedoes fell away quickly and so the Ju 88s resorted to flying
high-altitude missions at dusk, dropping fragmentation bombs. Losses
were high.

Through the spring of 1944, the Ju 88 torpedo-carriers of KGs 26
and 77 continued to be a thorn in the side of Allied shipping in both the
Mediterranean and in the Arctic, albeit with diminishing success because
of the continuing increase in enemy tonnage, warships and aircraft.

Typical of such activity was the mission flown by around 20 Ju 88A-17s
of I. and III./KG 77 in the early hours of 1 April against the American
convoy UGS-36 en route from Hampton Roads, Virginia, to Port Said,
Egypt. The bombers struck the convoy west of Algiers, with torpedoes
narrowly missing the Liberty ship SS *Marion McKinley Bovard* by just
75-100 yards. The 7180-GRT SS *Jared Ingersoll* (also a Liberty ship),
carrying stores and petrol, was not so lucky, being damaged when it was
hit by a torpedo at 0400 hrs. Fire broke out on board the vessel and it
was abandoned by the crew, who were rescued by the destroyer escort
USS *Mills* (DE-383). That vessel and the tug HMS *Mindful* towed the
ship to Algiers, where it was beached. SS *Jared Ingersoll* was later repaired
and returned to service.

This success had come at a price for the attackers, however, as three
Ju 88s were lost in the action as a result of defensive fire, including one
shot down by SS *Jared Ingersoll*.

On the night of 11/12 April, another formation of around 20 Ju 88s
from I. and III./KG 77 attacked again, this time the target being the
102 merchantmen of UGS-37 bound for Port Said with their 19 escorts.
The Junkers reached the convoy just before midnight, 56 km east of
Algiers, and had to make their attack through dense anti-aircraft fire. One

torpedo narrowly crossed astern of the liberty ship SS *Horace H Lurton* while another struck the destroyer escort USS *Holder* (DE-401) amidships on the port side, causing two large explosions. Despite fire breaking out on board and serious flooding, the crew remained at their posts and continued to fight off the Ju 88s. *Holder* was eventually towed to Oran and then on to New York, where it was deemed to be irreparable and scrapped. Seven Ju 88A-17s were in turn lost on this mission.

With the coming of the Allied landings in Normandy on 6 June 1944, III./KG 26 and I. and III./KG 77 quickly left their southern French bases for the Invasion front. Less than 24 hours after the first troops had come ashore, these units were attacking the landing fleet off the Cherbourg Peninsula. For the next three months, the *Gruppen* maintained determined, if sporadic, operations against enemy warships and supply vessels, but with little success. On the night of 13/14 June, two torpedoes launched by Ju 88s from KG 77 sank the destroyer HMS *Boadicea* as it escorted a westbound convoy off Portland. One of the torpedoes detonated the ship's magazine and it sank rapidly, with only 12 survivors from a complement of 182.

On the 18th, the Luftwaffe sent up no fewer than 69 aircraft armed with torpedoes and mines to strike at enemy shipping. The 1760-GRT Canadian-built British supply ship *Albert C Field*, carrying 2500 tons of munitions and 1300 sacks of post bound for Normandy, was struck by a torpedo launched by a Ju 88. According to the vessel's First Officer;

'At 2340 on 18 June 1944, when in position off St Catherine's Point, steering a course south at six knots, we were struck by one torpedo from an aircraft. The weather was fine and clear, visibility good. No one saw the track of the torpedo which struck our starboard side, amidships, on a bulkhead separating our two holds. The explosion was dull, like a very heavy depth charge, no water was thrown up and no flash was seen.'

Albert C Field sank within three minutes approximately ten miles southeast of Anvil Point.

On 8 August Hauptmann Siegfried Betke of 9./KG 26 was awarded the Knight's Cross and became a 'torpedo ace'. His record for anti-shipping missions stretched back to 1942 and operations against British shipping off the southern coast of Ireland and the west of England with 9./KG 77. He later flew against Malta and Allied convoys in the Mediterranean, as well as conducting bombing missions over North Africa. After a period of torpedo training on the Baltic coast in late 1943, he returned to the Mediterranean with 9./KG 26, flying the Ju 88A-17 against convoys off North Africa, before being relocated to France for attacks against the *Overlord* landing fleet. Betke became a recipient of the Knight's Cross for his success and leadership of torpedo operations. By war's end he had flown 190 combat missions and sunk six merchantmen, with damage inflicted on many others.

Another pilot to be recognised as a *Torpedoflieger* was Major Willi Sölter, who joined the Luftwaffe in 1937. A veteran of the Mediterranean campaign with I./KG 77, of which he was appointed *Kommandeur* on 1 July 1943, he flew many missions against convoys and individual ships in the south and then off Normandy, where he was credited with the sinking of a destroyer. After I./KG 77 was redesignated as I./KG 26 in July 1944,

Sölter was awarded the Knight's Cross on 8 August. The following month he moved to Bardufoss, in Norway, where his *Gruppe* conducted operations against enemy convoys in the Arctic.

In the south of France on 15 August, after Allied forces had landed along the coast between Cannes and Hyères in Operation *Dragoon*, individual Ju 88s from III./KG 26 attempted to attack the landing fleet with torpedoes, but failed.

On 6 October the *Kommodore* of KG 77, Wilhelm Stemmler, received the Knight's Cross for his leadership of the *Geschwader*. The following month he took command of KG 26, operating against the Arctic convoys. He would fill this position until the end of the war.

All the torpedo *Gruppen* flew on until VE Day, operating mainly against convoys in the Far North, but worsening weather, poor serviceability, a lack of torpedoes, their failures and heavy losses conspired to erode their effectiveness significantly.

The *Staffelkapitän* of 9./NJG 2, Oberleutnant Heinrich *Prinz* zu Sayn-Wittgenstein (left), stands by the rudder of his Ju 88C-6 nightfighter R4+ET at Gilze-Rijen in the autumn of 1942 for a photograph with his crew. The tail of the Junkers is marked with Sayn-Wittgenstein's 21 victories scored to that point, the last being a B-24 shot down over the southwest coast of the Netherlands on 10 September (*Author's collection*)

NIGHTFIGHTERS

There were relatively few pilots who transitioned from flying the Ju 88 as a bomber to flying it as a nightfighter in the nocturnal defence of the Reich, and also to have their combat records endorsed by the award of the Knight's Cross. One of the most famous of this select group was Major Heinrich *Prinz* zu Sayn-Wittgenstein, who was born in Copenhagen on 14 August 1916. His military career commenced in 1936 when he joined a cavalry regiment, but in the summer of the following year he transferred to the Luftwaffe. Sayn-Wittgenstein received initial flying instruction at Braunschweig, followed by bomber training on the He 111 at various schools before being commissioned as a Leutnant in June 1938 and posted to I./KG 54 at Fritzlar. It was not long before he was reassigned to 7./KG 1, with whom he would fly He 111s in the Western campaign until June 1940.

From mid-August he undertook missions over England, these being mainly night attacks on targets such as Biggin Hill, London, Coventry, Rochester and Derby. The following month, however, III./KG 1 began conversion to the Ju 88A-5, and in the early hours of 15 November, Sayn-Wittgenstein completed his first mission in this type – the infamous night attack on Coventry in which he recorded that his aircraft had to fly through heavy anti-aircraft fire and searchlight beams to drop 1500kg of bombs that fell on the assigned target. Returning to Montdidier, his *Gruppe*'s Ju 88s were serviced and loaded up again before heading out during the evening of the 15th to bomb London. Further missions were flown to the British capital and Birmingham.

RIGHT
Photographed in 1943, probably at Insterburg, Major *Prinz* zu Sayn-Wittgenstein briefs personnel of IV./NJG 5 ahead of a flight in his Ju 88C-6 C9+AE, which is seen behind him. Note the radar aerials protruding from above and below the wing, and the removal of the cabin's rear machine gun. This aircraft is also believed to have been fitted with a trial version of the obliquely-fitted, upward-firing *Schräge Musik* twin cannon installation in the upper fuselage (*Author's collection*)

Hauptmann Heinrich *Prinz* zu
Sayn-Wittgenstein walks one pace behind
Generalleutnant Josef Kammhuber at
Gilze-Rijen during the official presentation
of his Knight's Cross on 7 October 1942.
The ace had claimed his 22nd night victory
(almost certainly a Stirling of No 149 Sqn)
in the Ju 88 exactly three weeks earlier
(*Author's collection*)

For the launch of Operation *Barbarossa*, III./KG 1 was based at Eichwalde, in East Prussia, from where it carried out attacks on Libau and Riga/Spolva, then on enemy airfields. The *Gruppe* moved forward, behind the German advance in the northern sector of the front, to Mitau, Pleskau, Saborowka and had reached Dno by October.

At some stage in the autumn, Sayn-Wittgenstein was transferred to the southern sector to KG 51, but his posting there was to be brief for in January 1942 he volunteered for the nightfighter arm. It was to be a providential decision, for Sayn-Wittgenstein's career as a nightfighter pilot was to be meteoric. Initially assigned to 9./NJG 2 at Gilze-Rijen and appointed *Staffelkapitän* in November 1941, he transitioned relatively easily to the Ju 88C-6 nightfighter. The latter was a fundamental modification of the day fighter, usually painted black, with factory-installed flame-dampers and eventually the fitment of additional radio and radar equipment, with the nose-mounted aerials for the early FuG 202 *Lichtenstein* search radar adversely affecting speed. The C-6 was actually slower than the Lancasters and Halifaxes of RAF Bomber Command it was meant to shoot down!

Oberleutnant zu Sayn-Wittgenstein's first night victory was over a Blenheim of No 18 Sqn, which he shot down into the North Sea on the night of 6/7 May 1942. On 30/31 May he claimed a Wellington and a Manchester destroyed, and from then on he claimed regularly. Indeed, by the time Sayn-Wittgenstein was awarded the Knight's Cross on 2 October, his tally stood at 22 night victories. In February 1943, having failed to add any further kills to his score, Sayn-Wittgenstein returned to operations over the Eastern Front as *Kommandeur* of IV./NJG 5, based at Insterburg and equipped with the Bf 110 – he preferred, and retained, his Ju 88C-6, however. He resumed scoring on 16 April 1943 when he destroyed a Soviet DB-3 twin-engined bomber, and the highlight of his six-month tour in the East came on 20 July when he shot down seven bombers 15 km northeast of Orel – six of them in the space of 47 minutes. This remarkable accomplishment undoubtedly went a long way towards securing Sayn-Wittgenstein the Oak Leaves for the Knight's Cross on 31 August, when his score stood at 61 enemy aircraft confirmed destroyed.

This Ju 88G-6, coded 'A', was possibly assigned to II./NJG 3 at Grove, in Denmark, in 1944. The unit was commanded by Major Klaus Havenstein until September of that year, when he was succeeded upon his death in action by Hauptmann Werner Hüschens. The aircraft is fitted with FuG 220 *Lichtenstein* SN-2 antennae. Note also the single spiral on each spinner

Having returned to NJG 2 that same month, now Major Sayn-Wittgenstein was formally appointed *Kommodore* of the *Geschwader* at Deelan, in the Netherlands, on 1 January 1944. Heavily involved in the night war against RAF Bomber Command, Sayn-Wittgenstein marked his promotion the following night by downing six Lancasters in just over an hour as they approached the city of Berlin. These aircraft represented his 65th to 70th kills.

Just three weeks later, on 21 January, he was on course to repeat this astonishing run of success when he shot down three Lancasters and two Halifaxes of the RAF force out to bomb Magdeburg that night. It was as he was about to shoot down the last of these while to the east of the city that he was either hit by defensive fire or, more likely, by a burst of fire from beneath his Ju 88 from a Mosquito of No 141 Sqn. Feldwebel Friedrich Ostheimer, Sayn-Wittgenstein's radio operator, noted shortly after the mission;

'There were still further targets on my search radar. After a few alterations of course we saw yet another Lancaster. One attack left the machine with its fuselage on fire. The fire was getting smaller, and we began to make another attack. We were just in position, with Major Wittgenstein about to open fire, when there was a frightful cracking and flashing in our aircraft. Simultaneously, the port wing began to burn and the machine went into a dive. Then I saw the cabin roof above my head fly off and heard a shout – something like "*Get out!*" – on the intercom. I tugged my oxygen mask and headset off and was flung out of the aircraft. After a short time I pulled my ripcord and after about 15 minutes I came to the ground to the east of Hohengohrener Dam near Schönhausen. As far as I could tell we were attacked from below. I was unable to observe anything further. The crash occurred shortly before 2300 hrs.'

The *Prinz* was found dead the next morning in the wreckage of his aircraft in forested countryside in the area of Stendal, some 90 km north of Magdeburg.

Major Heinrich *Prinz* zu Sayn-Wittgenstein's final victory score stands at 79 (of which 33 were scored in the East), making him the third most successful Luftwaffe nightfighter pilot and the leading Ju 88 ace. Two days later, he was awarded the posthumous Swords to the Knight's Cross with Oak Leaves.

Leutnant Arnold Döring of 7./NJG 2 and 10./NJG 3 was one of the final nightfighter recipients of the Knight's Cross, being officially notified of his decoration on 17 April 1945. He did not receive the medal itself before the end of the war, however. Döring had flown the He 111 in Russia with KG 53, notching up an impressive tally of enemy trains and ships destroyed prior to transferring to the Defence of the Reich in early 1944 to fly with 7./JG 300. Döring had claimed five night and three day victories with this unit by the time he joined 7./NJG 2 in May 1944, where his previous twin-engined experience helped him convert to the Ju 88G. This *Staffel* was redesignated 10./NJG 3 in September and Döring would go on to score five night kills, two of which were claimed during Operation *Gisela* (a large-scale Luftwaffe night-intruder operation mounted over England) on the night of 3/4 March 1945. Döring is credited with flying 392 combat missions and scoring 23 victories, 13 of the latter at night

From 1 October 1943, Hauptmann Gerhard Raht from Reinfeld, in Schleswig-Holstein, was *Kapitän* of the Ju 88C-equipped 4./NJG 3. By the end of that year he was credited with 16 aerial victories, and on the night of 22/23 March 1944 he shot down four enemy bombers. Raht would go on to score multiple victories in one night on four more occasions. He ended the war with 58 night victories, by which time he had been appointed *Kommandeur* of I./NJG 2 and been awarded the Oak Leaves to the Knight's Cross

This Ju 88G of 2./NJG 4 is about to have its left engine warmed up prior to starting at Gütersloh, in Germany, in early 1945

In the spring of 1944, a new variant of Ju 88 began to reach the *Nachtjagdgeschwader* – the Ju 88G-1. Powered by BMW 801G radial engines, the G-1 was finished with the fuselage and more angular tail shape of the Ju 188 and the wings of the A-4. Armament consisted of four 20 mm MG 151 cannon in a ventral tray, providing formidable firepower for work against bombers, with a 13 mm MG 131 machine gun for the wireless operator. For target acquisition there was FuG 220 *Lichtenstein* SN-2 radar and a FuG 227 *Flensburg* passive radar receiver to home onto emissions from the British *Monica* tail warning radar. The G-1 was the first in a series of ongoing developments for this dedicated nightfighter variant, and by August 1944, such aircraft were on the strength of NJGs 1, 2, 3, 4, 5 and 6, I./NJG 7 and I./NJG 100.

Among the most successful aces to fly the Ju 88G exclusively was Hauptmann Heinz Rökker of I./NJG 2 who is credited with 61 victories scored at night over the Mediterranean, North Africa and northwest Europe (his career details appear in Chapter 2). He was awarded the Oak Leaves to the Knight's Cross on 12 March 1945. Hauptmann Gerhard Raht flew with NJG 3 and NJG 2, claiming 58 night victories over 171 missions, while Leutnant Arnold Döring of III./NJG 2 and 10./NJG 3 accounted for the greater part of his 13 nocturnal victories while flying the Ju 88 from May 1944.

Finally, as an example of the relatively unsung Ju 88 aces who flew from beginning to end, by day and night, as a bomber pilot and a nightfighter pilot, there was Oberfeldwebel Eduard Lindinger from Sattlern in Bavaria. Born on 17 January 1915, Lindinger joined the Luftwaffe in November 1937 and after a standard route through flying and bomber training, was posted in June 1940 to 7./KG 1, where one of his *Staffel* officers was Leutnant Heinrich *Prinz* zu Sayn-Wittgenstein. After flying missions in the He 111 over France and England, III./KG 1 then took part in operations over the northern flank of the Eastern Front. Feldwebel Lindinger flew regular missions attacking factories and other strategic targets, as well as accounting for eight tanks, three locomotives, three trains and more than 100 trucks, He also sank three Russian naval vessels.

On 3 August 1942, by which time Lindinger had flown more than 280 combat missions in the East, he was shot down by Soviet fighters while attacking an enemy minesweeper in the Gulf of Finland. He and all other members of his crew were seriously wounded. The award of the Knight's Cross came while he was still recovering in hospital. For the latter half of 1943

and the first half of 1944, Lindinger carried out various instructor roles, as well as some test-flying at the armament *Erprobungsstelle* at Tarnewitz, but with the worsening state of the war, in August 1944 he volunteered for nightfighters. He was posted to III./NJG 5 under the command of ace Major Paul Zorner, where he flew the Ju 88G on several operational sorties until war's end. Oberfeldwebel Lindinger is known to have flown 322 combat missions.

'ADLER' GESCHWADER

We end where we began – with I./KG 30. Throughout the war the *'Adler' Geschwader* had flown the Ju 88 exclusively as a bomber, from Norway and the Arctic to the Mediterranean. By the time of the Allied landings in Normandy in June 1944, its I., II. and III. *Gruppen* were back in Germany, with IV./KG 30 at Aalborg.

Commanding I./KG 30 was Hauptmann Erich Baumgartl. An Eastern Front veteran, Baumgartl had flown missions in He 111s of 3./KG 55 in support of German forces at Stalingrad. Awarded the Knight's Cross on 31 July 1943, he converted to the Ju 88 and undertook missions over Italy with III./LG 1, being appointed *Kommandeur* of I./KG 30 on 17 February 1944. His new *Gruppe* had carried out bombing raids on London as part of Operation *Steinbock* in January 1944, before being transferred to Bergamo, in Italy, where it was used to attack Allied forces landing at Anzio-Nettuno. The *Gruppe* then returned to the Reich in March to re-equip and train up on the new Ju 88S-3, which would become the last production Ju 88 bomber.

Built in limited numbers, with priority by this stage having gone over to nightfighters, the S series was recognisable by its smooth, rounded, glazed nose that replaced the 'beetle's eye' of earlier variants. The S-3 was powered by Jumo 213A 12-cylinder, liquid-cooled, inline engines with GM-1 nitrous oxide injection to boost take-off power. In addition to a few examples going to I./KG 30, small numbers were also delivered to I./KG 66 and II./KG 200.

During May 1944 and into early June, in anticipation of the Allied landings, some sporadic bombing raids were carried out by I./KG 30 on coastal targets in England, such as naval installations at Portsmouth. When *Overlord* finally did materialise, the Ju 88s were hurled into operations over the Invasion front, Normandy and northern France. On one of the first missions, on the night of 11/12 July, Hauptmann Baumgartl was shot down and killed when his S-3 was attacked by a British nightfighter near Rouen. Only his radio operator managed to bail out. Baumgartl had accumulated 350 combat missions.

The surviving records of the *Gruppe*'s 3. *Staffel* under Hauptmann Fritz Hasselbeck show that it spent July, August and up to mid-September 1944 using its Ju 88S-3s and a few remaining A-4s in night missions from Le Culot, Orly, Montdidier and Quackenbrück, mining the Seine estuary and bombing the beachhead areas. Then, as German forces began their inexorable retreat east, 3./KG 30's crews attacked towns such as St Lô and Avranches, the Meuse canal and Eindhoven, as well as Allied troop columns, assembly areas and armoured groupings with SC- and SD-500s

Hauptmann Martin Becker was a former reconnaissance pilot who transferred to the nightfighter arm in 1943, joining 11./NJG 4. After this *Staffel* was redesignated 2./NJG 6, Becker was appointed as *Staffelkapitän* on 17 October 1943, by which point he had scored his first night victory. From then until March 1945, his score would rise dramatically. On the night of 14/15 March 1945, Becker and his radio-operator Leutnant Karl-Ludwig Johanssen shot down eight RAF Lancasters and a Fortress II (the latter from special operations ECM unit No 214 Sqn). It was a record score for one night, and Becker was awarded the Oak Leaves to his Knight's Cross on 20 March – Johanssen was awarded the Knight's Cross that same day. Becker ended the war with 58 victories to his name, virtually all of them in the Ju 88

RIGHT
Destined for the scrap heap, single Ju 88A bomber 4D+BW of KG 30, with a large '77' on its tail assembly, is parked among a line-up of Ju 88G and Bf 110G nightfighters in an aircraft park somewhere in Germany shortly after the end of the war. Cockpits and engines have been protected by tarpaulins, but all propellers have been removed. Note the wide variation in camouflage on the Ju 88s (*Author's collection*)

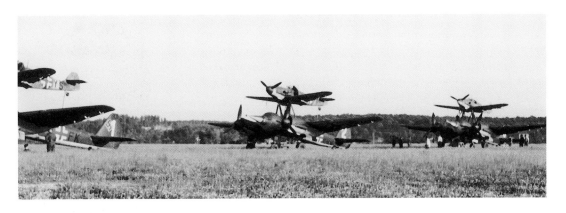

An inglorious end. Three mission-ready, war-weary Ju 88A airframes, converted into 'fly and forget' bombs through the fitting of a hollow charge warhead packed with 1700 kg of explosive as the lower component of the *Mistel* S1 composite aircraft, of the *Einsatzstaffel*/KG 101 have been carefully towed out onto the runway at St Dizier in the summer of 1944. Flown from the upper Bf 109 fighter by pilots who, in the main had come from bomber units, these aircraft were deployed unsuccessfully against the Allied invasion fleet off Normandy in 1944 and then in greater numbers against the bridges over the Oder River in 1945 (*Author's collection*)

and SD- and AB-70 containers loaded with SD-1 'butterfly' anti-personnel bombs, often flying two missions in one night.

Losses to Allied nightfighters and anti-aircraft defences were draining and became unsustainable. Hasselbeck went missing in action on 11 July during a minelaying sortie over the Seine, and his body was washed ashore near Dieppe. His replacement was a young Austrian arrival, Oberleutnant Rudolf Kainz.

But there was little the bombers could do and their efforts, in reality, were a nuisance to the Allies rather than a threat. One by one, pilots from 3./KG 30 and many other bomber *Staffeln* like them became redundant across the airfields in the Reich until they were found a new use as hastily-trained jet-bomber pilots in *Kampfgeschwader* (*Jagd*) (Bomber Units Converted to Fighter Deployment). In the case of the 'new' 3./KG(J) 30, pilots controlled *Mistel* composite aircraft in which a Ju 88 fuselage with its cockpit removed and replaced by a massive hollow-charge warhead was flown by a Bf 109 or Fw 190 perched atop at bridges over rivers in the East as a last-ditch attempt to hold back the Russians. But that is another story.

COLOUR PLATES

1

Ju 88A-1 Wk-Nr 299 9K+HS of III./KG 51, Etampes-Mondésir, France, summer 1940

One of the early Ju 88s to be taken on by III./KG 51 following the *Gruppe*'s conversion to the type from the He 111 in June 1940, this aircraft is finished in a standard splinter pattern of RLM 70/71, with the bomber's individual letter 'H' in red, outlined in white. The aircraft carried the *Geschwader*'s Edelweiss emblem in the usual location beneath the cockpit.

2

Ju 88A-1 4D+CR of 1./KG 30, Oldenburg, Germany, May 1940

A typical aircraft of 1./KG 30 of the 1940 period, this Ju 88A-1 is also camouflaged in a standard splinter pattern of RLM 70/71. The bomber's individual letter 'C' is in white, and the *Geschwader*'s diving eagle emblem can be clearly seen between the glazed nose and the cockpit. 1. *Staffel* was unique in that its aircraft carried the unit emblem, depicting Neville Chamberlain's umbrella in a gunsight, on the outer sides of the engine nacelles.

3

Ju 88A-4 B3+BM of 4./KG 54, Saint-André-de-l'Eure, France, August 1940

Finished in a standard splinter pattern of RLM 70/71, this KG 54 Ju 88 carried the Death's Head *Geschwader* emblem beneath the cockpit in white (obscured here by the port engine), as well as II. *Gruppe*'s red diagonal band forward of the fuselage code.

4

Ju 88A-5 Wk-Nr 4219 of an unknown *Staffel* from KG 30, possibly Gilze-Rijen, the Netherlands, late 1940/early 1941

For night-bombing missions over the British Isles in late 1940/41, this aircraft has had temporary sooty black distemper applied to its undersides, fuselage sides, spinners and tail fin, with all but its *Werknummer* and the merest trace of its fuselage code visible.

5

Ju 88A-5 L1+GH flown by Oberfelwebel Otto Leupert, I./LG 1, Benghazi-Benina, Libya, October 1941

This Junkers was finished in a plain covering of RLM 79 *Sandgelb* on upper and fuselage services, while the undersides were RLM 65 *Hellblau*, for operations over North Africa and the Mediterranean. The aircraft also carried a white theatre fuselage band and the red griffon emblem of *Lehrgeschwader* 1 on a white shield between the cockpit and the glazed nose. The spinners were in red and white half segments.

6

Ju 88A-5 F1+JR of 7./KG 76, Rakopolje, Russia, autumn 1941

Aircraft of 7. *Staffel* were noteworthy for the narrow white identification band which their aircraft carried just forward of the fuselage code and the yellow theatre band that was applied directly beneath the *Balkenkreuz*, rather than aft of it as was usually the case. This Ju 88 had the last three digits of its Werknummer applied to the upper tail fin, while the aircraft's individual letter 'J' and spinner tips were in white.

7

Ju 88A-4 trop L1+HK of 2./LG 1, Derna, Libya, December 1941

Several aircraft flown by LG 1 in North Africa had a camouflage of random spots of RLM 80 or 81 applied over a base of RLM 79. This aircraft was otherwise void of unit insignia except for its national markings, fuselage code and white Mediterranean theatre fuselage band. The aircraft letter 'H', in black along with the rest of the code, was not applied over the band.

8

Ju 88A-4 F1+AS of 8./KG 76, Orscha-Süd, Russia, December 1941

The Luftwaffe applied a temporary white finish to many of its aircraft operating during the winter months on the Russian Front. This Ju 88 of 8./KG 76 has its uppersurfaces in white, while the undersurfaces retain the original RLM 65. The unit code is in black, but the aircraft letter 'A' is in red, outlined in white, and the spinners also have red tips with a soft demarcation line with the white. The aircraft also carried the *Staffel* emblem of a wasp with silver wings on a red disc beneath the cockpit.

9

Ju 88C R4+C? of I./NJG 2, Gilze-Rijen, the Netherlands, late 1941/early 1942

This nightfighter of NJG 2 has had black paint applied crudely, with wide brush strokes, to its undersides, fuselage sides and tail unit, while its uppersurfaces retain the original RLM 70/71 splinter pattern. All national and unit markings have been covered, leaving only the 'Englandblitz' emblem of the *Nachtjagd*, depicting an eagle diving at a map of the British Isles set against a red lightning flash, beneath the cockpit and the aircraft's identification letter, which is also probably black, outlined in white.

10

Ju 88C-4 Wk-Nr 360219 R4+GM flown by Oberfeldwebel Wilhelm Beier, 4./NJG 2, Gilze-Rijen, the Netherlands, summer 1942

Beier's C-4 is finished in overall RLM 74 Dunkelgrau, although the undersides are in a lighter grey-blue. The aircraft code is in matt black apart from the aircraft letter G, which is in black outlined in white. The Balkenkreuz has been muted by crudely applied brush strokes of black paint. The tailfin is marked with 22 of Oberfeldwebel Beier's eventual 36 night victories. It is possible that the 'Englandblitz' emblem of the *Nachtjagd* was applied to the nose.

11

Ju 88A-4 R4+DK of I./NJG 2, Catania, Sicily, 1942

Most of this A-4, which was one of a small number used by I./NJG 2 for nocturnal bombing missions, was painted in black, but the engine units with cowlings may have been replacements and were finished in RLM 70/71 day camouflage. The fuselage theatre band was in white, with the code in grey. The engine undersides were dirty and oil-stained. It is possible that the 'Englandblitz' emblem of the *Nachtjagd* was applied to the nose.

12

Ju 88C-6 R4+HH of 1./NJG 2, Catania, Sicily, 1942

Finished in overall matt black, this C-6 was similar to A-4 R4+DK but with the white theatre band applied further forward and the unit's numeral duly painted over it. The aircraft is also adorned with three victory markings, at least two of which are believed to be credited to Oberleutnant Gerhard Böhme. It is possible that the 'Englandblitz' emblem of the *Nachtjagd* was applied to the nose.

13

Ju 88C-4 R4+MT of 9./NJG 2, Gilze-Rijen, the Netherlands, summer 1942

A rarely seen nightfighter finished in standard RLM 70/71 splinter pattern, this Ju 88 had a Balkenkreuz outlined thinly in black and its individual aircraft letter, M, outlined in a muted white. The 'Englandblitz' emblem of the *Nachtjagd* was also applied to the nose.

14

Ju 88A-4 Wk-Nr 1016 3Z+DB flown by Leutnant Johannes Geismann, I./KG 77, Catania, Sicily, mid-1942

Geismann's Ju 88 was finished in an RLM 70/71 splinter pattern, with three of its code letters in a muted matt black, and the aircraft letter, D, in an unusual lined style. In addition to a *Hakenkreuz* (swastika), the aircraft's tail carried a four-digit Werknummer and single victory bar denoting a British fighter shot down on 16 October 1942. The crowing cockerel emblem of I./KG 77, in the old German national colours of red, yellow and black, adorns the top of the rudder, which is also decorated with ten ship silhouettes. Each of these carries a British roundel on its hull, the date of sinking, the vessel's tonnage (GRT) and a 'V' for '*versenkt*' (sunk).

15

Ju 88A-4 Trop B3+LH of I./KG 54, Tympakion, Crete, June 1942

This Junkers is finished in an overall coating of Sandgelb for tropical service. Its fuselage carries the white Mediterranean theatre band at the rear and the code is in black, except the aircraft letter, L, which is in yellow, outlined thinly in black. The spinners are in a dark green, tipped in the *Staffel* colour of white. The nose is marked with the last two digits of the Werknummer, '72', and the underside colour of RLM 65 light blue extends almost up to the engine exhausts. It is possible the aircraft may have been recoded, as the outer wing underside bears a patch of new paint outboard of the national cross.

16

Ju 88A-4 M2+AK of 2./KGr.106, Dinard, France, 1942

A very faded RLM 70/71 pattern adorns this Ju 88, which has also had its markings obscured for night-bombing operations (some of this has worn off the Balkenkreuz) and its undersides finished in temporary black. The *Gruppe* had been formed in February 1941 from Kü.Fl.Gr.106, and it operated over Britain from that month to August 1942, deploying A-4s, A-5s, A-6s and D-1s.

17

Ju 88C-4 R4+FM flown by Leutnant Wilhelm Beier, 10./NJG 1, Leeuwarden, the Netherlands, October 1942

The aircraft appears to have retained an RLM 70/71 pattern on the fuselage and uppersurfaces, but with crudely applied black to the undersides. Beier's 36 victories are shown in bars on the base of the tail fin, which extend over the Hakenkreuz. To the right of the victory bars is a small rendition of a Knight's Cross, which Beier had been awarded on 11 October 1941 in recognition of 14 nocturnal kills. It is also believed that this Junkers carried the 'Englandblitz' emblem of the *Nachtjagd* beneath the cockpit – it is obscured from view by the port engine.

18

Ju 88A-4 V4+FH of I./KG 1, Charkow-Woitschenko, Russia, winter 1942/43

This aircraft of KG 1 has received a temporary wash of white paint that has begun to wear. The undersides of the wingtips and engines, as well as the fuselage band, are in the Eastern Front theatre colour of yellow, while the code is in black. The spinner tips have also had white applied, but the original red is now showing through. A small black repair patch appears on the fuselage band.

19

Ju 88C-6 F1+KT flown by Oberleutnant Dieter Lukesch, 9./KG 76, Catania, Sicily, May 1943

The base Sandgelb colour on this C-6 has been sprayed with a dark green random scribble pattern camouflage. The aircraft's fuselage band, individual letter and spinner tips are in white. III./KG 76 had several C-6s on strength in the Mediterranean during this period, with this one being regularly flown by Knight's Cross holder Oberleutnant Dieter Lukesch.

20

Ju 88D-1 F6+DN of 5.(F)/*Aufklärungsgruppe* 122, Gosstkino, Russia, early 1943

Operating in the harsh winter conditions of the Leningrad Front, this D-1 reconnaissance machine has been camouflaged appropriately. However, there is a strong demarcation line between the temporary white on the fuselage sides and the pale blue of the undersides. The white on the uppersurfaces of the engine nacelles has virtually disappeared and the spinners are in the 5. *Staffel* colour of red

21
Ju 88A-4 5K+FN of II./KG 3, Poltava, Russia, summer 1943

An aircraft truly representative of many Ju 88s in service in Russia, this bomber is finished in a standard RLM 70/71 splinter pattern and has bright yellow fuselage theatre band. The aircraft would have been adorned with the emblem of II./KG 3, comprising a stylised lightning flash in white against a red shield, beneath the cockpit – again, this is obscured by the starboard engine. The spinners were painted in black, green and red, while the fuselage code appears to have been applied in a muted shade of dark grey.

22
Ju 88C-6 F8+RY of 14./KG 40, Lorient, France, autumn 1943

This C-6 of V./KG 40 has received the revised pale blue/grey scheme that began to appear on several of the *Gruppe's* aircraft from the summer of 1943, and which was intended for overwater operations. The fuselage sides, engine undersides, spinners and tail assembly were finished in a single overall colour, probably RLM 76 or 77, while the wing and fuselage uppersurfaces were given thick random streaks of RLM 74 that extended over the upper nacelles of the engines. Three letters of the fuselage codes were in a muted grey, but the aircraft's individual letter, R, was in black with no outline.

23
Ju 88C-6 Wk-Nr 3060381 F8+BX of 13./KG 40, Lorient, France, September 1943

Despite a revised scheme being adopted for several of the *Gruppe's* aircraft, as per the Ju 88C-6 in the previous profile, many of the machines flown by V./KG 40 continued to be camouflaged in an RLM 70/71 pattern through to the end of 1943.

24
Ju 88A-4 3Z+AH of 1./KG 77, Orange-Caritat, France, spring/summer 1944

Ranging over the Mediterranean and the coast of North Africa against Allied shipping targets from its base at Orange-Caritat, in the south of France, this Ju 88 has had its RLM 70/71 splinter oversprayed with a random scribble pattern, probably of RLM 77. Furthermore, the white of the fuselage Balkenkreuz and theatre band and the Hakenkreuz have been crudely masked in temporary black. The undersides appear to have been painted in black as well, suggesting night missions.

25
Ju 88A-4 3Z+EH of I./KG 77, Orange-Caritat, France, spring/summer 1944

As with the Ju 88A-4 in the previous profile, this aircraft has been subjected to a crude, in-the-field overspray scribble. The white of the fuselage Balkenkreuz and theatre band and the Hakenkreuz have been crudely brushed over in temporary black, and the visibility of the aircraft letter E has been heightened by its rough outlining in white. The aircraft undersides have also been heavily stippled in a temporary black.

26
Ju 88A-4 3Z+KS of 8./KG 77, Orange-Caritat, France, spring/summer 1944

Another variation of overwater camouflage used by KG 77, this time on an aircraft of III. *Gruppe*, was the 'wave mirror' type. The base RLM 70/71 scheme has been densely covered in a pattern of horizontal 'wave' scribbles running the length of the aircraft and over the wings and nacelles. While the code letters seem muted, the edges of the Balkenkreuz appear to have been repainted in bold white.

27
Ju 88A-4 L1+BM of 4./LG 1, Glize-Rijen, the Netherlands, June 1944

Aircraft of II./LG 1 retained a scribble pattern as used in the Mediterranean when they were transferred to the Netherlands from Italy in June 1944 in response to Operation *Overlord*. The rear fuselage band appears to be in the same colour as the scribble (RLM 77), while the aircraft letter B is in black, outlined in white.

28
Ju 88G-6 C9+AC of Major Hans Leickhardt, *Kommandeur* of II./NJG 5, Stubendorf, Germany, autumn 1944

This G-6 nightfighter was finished originally in an overall colour of mid-grey RLM 75, but it was then oversprayed with RLM 76, although patches of the 75 were left visible. This aircraft was one of the few G-6s fitted with the *Morgenstern* (Morningstar) antenna for the FuG 220 *Lichtenstein* SN-2 radar to see combat. It also had the FuG 220's tail-warning radar installed, the system's distinctive antenna array protruding from the rear fuselage of the nightfighter

29
Ju 88G-6b D5+AE of Major Berthold Ney, *Kommandeur* of IV./NJG 3, Jever or Nordholz, Germany, early 1945

A mottle of RLM 74 has been sprayed over the fuselage base colour of light grey (possibly Hellgrau) along the top side and over the upper engine nacelles. A *Kommandeur's* chevron was applied well forward of the Balkenkreuz. The aircraft was fitted with FuG 220 Lichtenstein radar in the nose and it also had a tail-warning radar antenna array. Twin MG 151 *Schräge Musik* cannon were installed in the upper fuselage.

30
Ju 88G-1 4D+FK *Mistel* of II./KG(J) 30, Oranienburg, Germany, April 1945

An inglorious end. This Ju 88G-1 nightfighter airframe was converted into a *Mistel* composite lower component and fitted with an SHL 3500 hollow-charge warhead for operations by KG(J) 30 against bridge targets along the Oder River in April 1945.

SOURCES AND BIBLIOGRAPHY

BOOKS

Baumbach, Werner, *Broken Swastika – The Defeat of the Luftwaffe*, Robert Hale, London (1986)

Bergström, Christer, and Mikhailov, Andrey, *Black Cross-Red Star – The Air War over the Eastern Front, Volume 1: Operation Barbarossa, 1941*, Pacifica Military History, Pacifica (2000)

Boiten, Dr Theo E. W., *Nachtjagd War Diaries – An Operational History of the German Night Fighter Force in the West: Volume One, September 1939-March 1944*, Red Kite, Walton on Thames (2008)

Brütting, Georg, *Das waren die deutschen Kampfflieger Asse 1939-1945*, Motorbuch Verlag, Stuttgart (1975)

Budraß, Lutz, *Flugzeugindustrie und Luftrüstung in Deutschland 1918-1945*, Droste Verlag, Düsseldorf (1998)

Claasen, Adam R. A., *Hitler's Northern War – The Luftwaffe's Ill-Fated Campaign, 1940-1945*, University Press of Kansas, Lawrence (2001)

Dellmensingen, Obst i.G. a.D., Erhard Krafft v., *Das Kampfgeschwader 54 und die Kampfgruppe 806: Eine Chronik aus Berichten und Dokumenten aus den Jahren 1936-1945*, unpublished, 198?

Dierich, Wolfgang, *Kampfgeschwader 'Edelweiss': The History of a German Bomber Unit 1939-1945*, Ian Allan, Shepperton (1975)

Filley, Brian, *Junkers Ju 88 in Action, Part 1*, Squadron/Signal Publications, Carrolton (1988)

Goss, Chris, *Bloody Biscay – The History of V. Gruppe/Kampfgeschwader 40*, Crecy Publishing (1997)

Goss, Chris, *Sea Eagles Volume Two: Luftwaffe Anti-Shipping Units 1942-45*, Classic Publications, Hersham (2006)

Goss, Chris, *Junkers Ju 88: The Early Years – Blitzkrieg to the Blitz*, Frontline Books, Barnsley (2017)

Gundelach, Karl, *Die deutsche Luftwaffe im Mittelmeer 1940-1945 Band 1*, Peter D Lang, Frankfurt-am-Main (1981)

Gundelach, Karl, *Die deutsche Luftwaffe im Mittelmeer 1940-1945 Band 2*, Peter D. Lang, Frankfurt-am-Main (1981)

Homze, Edward L, *Arming the Luftwaffe*, University of Nebraska Press, Lincoln (1996)

Horn, Jan, *Wir flogen gen Westen: Die Chronik des Kampfgeschwaders 6 der deutschen Luftwaffe 1941-1945*, published privately, Dresden (2004)

Kainz, Rudi, *Geschichte der 3.Staffel, Kampfgeschwader 30*, private Chronik, Wien (1991)

Kaiser, Jochen, *Die Ritterkreuzträger der Kampfflieger – Band 1*, Luftfahrtverlag-Start, Bad Zwischenahn (2010)

Kaiser, Jochen, *Die Ritterkreuzträger der Kampfflieger – Band 2*, Luftfahrtverlag-Start, Bad Zwischenahn (2011)

Kay, Antony L, *Junkers Aircraft & Engines 1913-1945*, Putnam Aeronautical Books, London (2004)

Knott, Claire Rose, *Princes of Darkness: The lives of Luftwaffe night fighter aces Heinrich Prinz zu Sayn-Wittgenstein and Egmont Prinz zur Lippe-Weissenfeld*, Classic Publications, Hersham (2008)

Neitzel, Sönke, *Der Einsatz der deutschen Luftwaffe über dem Atlantik und der Nordsee 1939-1945*, Bernard & Graefe Verlag, Bonn (1995)

Parry, Simon W., *Intruders over Britain: The Luftwaffe Night Fighter Offensive 1940-45*, Air Research Publications, Surbiton (1987)

Radtke, Siegfried, *Kampfgeschwader 54 – Von der Ju 52 zur Me 262: Eine Chronik nach Kriegstagebüchern, Dokumenten und Berichten 1935-1945*, Schild Verlag, München (1990)

Reiche, Helmut, *Kampfeinsätze der "Helbig-Flyers" 1944/45: Erinnerungen eines Zeitzeugen der Kriegsgeneration*, VDM Heinz Nickel, Zweibrücken (2000)

Roskill, Captain S. W., *The War at Sea 1939-1945 – Volume I: The Defensive*, The Naval & Military Press Ltd, Uckfield (2004)

Smith, J. Richard, and Creek, Eddie J., *Kampfflieger Volume One: Bombers of the Luftwaffe 1933-1940*, Classic Publications, Hersham (2004)

Steenbeck, Alexander, *Die Spur des Löwen: der Weg des Löwengeschwaders durch Europa*, privately published, Lübeck (2012)

Taghon, Peter, *Die Geschichte des Lehrgeschwaders 1: Band 1 1936-1942*, VDM Heinz Nickel, Zweibrücken (2004)

Taghon, Peter, *Die Geschichte des Lehrgeschwaders 1: Band 2 1942-1945*, VDM Heinz Nickel, Zweibrücken (2004)

Thiele, Harold, *Luftwaffe Aerial Torpedo Aircraft and Operations in World War Two*, Hikoki Publications, Crowborough (2004)

Wadman, David, *Aufklärer – Luftwaffe Reconnaissance Aircraft and Units 1942-1945, Volume Two*, Classic Publications, Hersham (2007)

Wagner, Wolfgang, *Hugo Junkers – Pionier der Luftfahrt – seine Flugzeuge*, Bernard & Graefe, Bonn (1996)

de Zeng IV, Henry L., and Stankey, Douglas G., *Bomber Units of the Luftwaffe 1933-1945 – A Reference Source, Volume 1*, Midland Publishing, Hinckley (2007)

de Zeng IV, Henry L., and Stankey, Douglas G., *Bomber Units of the Luftwaffe 1933-1945 – A Reference Source, Volume 2*, Classic Publications, Hersham (2008)

Zindel, Ernst, *Die Geschichte und Entwicklung des Junkers-Flugzeugbaus von 1910 bis 1945 und bis zum endgültigen Ende 1970*, Deutsche Gesellschaft für Luft-und Raumfahrt, Köln (1979)

WEBSITES

The Luftwaffe 1933-1945 at www.w2.dk

War Diary German Naval Staff Operations Division Part A Volume 7, March 1940 accessed May 2018 at https://ia801603.us.archive.org/27/items/wardiarygermanna71940germ/wardiarygermanna71940germ.pdf

de Zeng IV, Henry L. & Stankey, Douglas G., *Luftwaffe Officer Career Summaries* (Version 1 April 2015) at www.ww2.dk/lwoffz.html

INDEX

Page numbers in **bold** refer to illustrations and their captions